BERTUS BASSON

HOMEGROWN

BERTUS BASSON

with Russel Wasserfall & Roxy Spears
Photography by Claire Gunn

FOREWORD

These days, if you're a chef, people are always asking when your cookbook's coming out. It's what you do. Open a restaurant, do your best to make a name for yourself, bring out a cookbook. Patrons ask for recipes for this or that, or they want a souvenir of their meal with us. This isn't really that kind of a cookbook.

There are one or two classic Overture recipes in these pages. There are a couple of recipes that have travelled with me, in one form or another, from kitchen to kitchen. Here and there are recipes that made me want to be a chef. Mostly, though, this book is about memories.

I guess I've resisted doing this for so long because once they are in a book, the recipes – the moment of creating that food – are frozen forever. It will always only be like that. Anyone who knows me at all, knows that I can never leave anything exactly as it is. I want to know how it can be better, or different, or more satisfying.

It's never cast in stone. If I do one thing with beetroot today, who's to say I won't taste something tomorrow that sends me in a whole new direction? What is cast in stone, though, is where I come from as a chef. The way I cook, the memories that make me pick up a beetroot, that is what drives the creative process.

In a sense, I see recipes as a sort of map of where I come from. That's really the idea behind *Homegrown*. If you thought it might be about growing your own spinach or living off the grid, you're going to be slightly disappointed. Our house is a bit like a farmyard with 3 dogs, a pig called Spek, a few hens and a veggie patch. We kind of want to live on a smallholding some day. But right now my wife Mareli and I love the excitement of creating and running restaurants.

We really do want to see what's around the next corner for us with food. I have been incredibly blessed in finding the perfect partner for this journey in Mareli. She is as curious about food, flavour and texture as I am. My wife is as happy sitting on a beer crate in a back street in Zanzibar slurping broth cooked by an old local lady as she is working through a scoop of the best gelato we've ever tasted from a tiny spot in San Gimignano in Tuscany.

The funny thing is, my perfect partner grew up right near me. I didn't have to work in London, compete for the SA team in the Culinary Olympics, and travel all over South Africa with a TV crew to meet her. She even went to the same school I did, right back home in Nelspruit.

Even though we never met back there and my family left for Cape Town when I was a teen, we share a lot of early memories of food. From peri-peri slap chips from the local Portuguese takeaway, to mealies cooked on the fire, chip 'n dip at braais and the all-consuming Sunday lunch tradition. She gets me. When I start fiddling with a flavour or an ingredient that lives in my memory but needs to be reborn on a fine-dining menu, Mareli gets it.

This book, *Homegrown*, is a look at how my food comes from those memories. It is about where my food journey began and how I draw on both my own memory and the strong cultural past of an Afrikaans kid to create the food in our restaurants. It's also about how I continue to make food memories all the time, immersing myself in the cultural diversity of South African cuisine. I do this because I love how we cook, but also because what we cook and how we eat as South Africans is such a rich fountain of inspiration.

This is not to say that we shouldn't look abroad for inspiration in our kitchens. I wouldn't even know where to start with sauces or complicated dishes without my training, rooted in the French culinary tradition. However, as much as it is about nourishment, food is also about sensory fulfilment. If a taste, smell, sound or texture can transport us to another place, a place of memory, that fulfilment can be made more complete.

It surprises friends to learn that I didn't like food as a kid. My mother, Hetta Basson (Ma), had to work hard to get me to eat anything that wasn't sweet or bad for me. I guess that's why my earliest food memories are of sweet things. In fact, this book starts with dessert. It's based on one of my most cherished childhood food memories. I remember the saying that used to go round: 'Life's uncertain. Eat your pudding first.' The ten-year-old me would definitely have agreed.

Ma's apple pudding is a staple in our restaurants. I even printed the recipe on a branded Bertus Basson tea towel. I play with other things that I learned from her, like when I turned melk tert into a soufflé at Overture, it was her melk tert filling I used as a base before going off-road. It became the most popular of all our desserts there. People still ask for it. In that way I worked with the iconic Afrikaans afternoon tea treat, and turned it into something I thought contemporary restaurant patrons would enjoy.

From my father, Theo Basson, I learned where meat actually comes from and why it should be treated with such respect. He would take us on hunting trips, or go off on his own to bring back something for the pot. From him I learned how to stretch the budget with ingredients for the restaurant from the veld or the ocean.

Another thing that comes from him is a no-nonsense approach to cooking. When he braais a snoek – one of his favourite culinary tasks – or cooks a chop on the fire, that's what it is. Snoek or a chop, simply but perfectly cooked. I take things like snoek, or the biltong he used to make in the garage, and play with those memories and techniques in my cooking. When I think of those things I also remember that food doesn't have to be fancy or over-worked, it just has to taste good.

I think many people look at TV cooking programmes and read all these cookbooks and think that's what cooking is. If they can do what some well-known chef is making, then they are better cooks. Are they? If you can cook like someone else, that's great. But they didn't teach you how to hold a spatula or crack an egg.

It's our own experience and interpretation or view of it that teaches us how to cook. The people you grew up with or learned to cook with taught you that stuff. Those memories, that flavour or smell living in your mind is what makes you the cook you are. I got all of that growing up. It is those memories and the path they led me down that drive me to constantly seek fresh experiences and experiment with new things.

Finally, no chef can cook without having someone to eat his food. I would be nowhere if it wasn't for all the people who've eaten my cooking. So I want to start by thanking every patron who has ever eaten in a restaurant where I've worked. Included in that group is every mate who's ever had a chop or a wors off one of my braais. Every sigh of satisfaction, every frown of criticism has made me a better chef.

There are colleagues who've shared the journey, side-by-side at the stove, or after a late shift over a coffee, with red eyes, working out ideas for the next service. You've all made this journey huge and wonderful.

Also in the enormous thank you bit is everyone who's ever shared a recipe or introduced me to a new food experience or technique. The obvious culprits here are my family. Ma and Dad I hope I remember to thank you in some way every time I see you for the building blocks you gave me for this life I live. My family includes my brother, oupa and ouma and all the aunts and uncles and cousins who were there around the table or in the kitchen whenever they needed to be.

Meeting and marrying my wife Mareli meant I inherited a whole new family from whom I continue to learn. Mareli added super-cool in-laws to my life, but also so much more. She is my life partner, my business partner and muse. She spent hours with me going over recipes and putting memories and history into a form that looked something like a book manuscript.

Anyone who knows chefs, knows that we are volatile and insecure and bombastic and all kinds of crazy rolled into one jumping bean. That's me. So some of you reading this will have an idea of how much kak Mareli has to put up with from her husband. Yet she does it all with such grace and patience. I hope I can come even a little way towards showing my deep and lasting appreciation for the amazing woman I married.

Homegrown wouldn't have come about without my friends Russel Wasserfall and his wife Camilla. Camilla is a truly inspirational cook, and it was Russel who chased me about the book and realised that it would need to be about place and past, capturing more than just a bunch of my recipes. He brought all the publishing bits together and teased out my voice in all the stories he's collected here.

The other patient and incredibly talented people in this little love circle are Roxy Spears and the photographer Claire Gunn. The two of them worked their butts off to make a kind of vague dream of a book into something real, and became like family in the process. Roxy is a true creative soul and Claire is a former chef, and they both just get me creatively.

From the kid who wouldn't eat his greens to juggling time between a bunch of restaurants and TV production schedules, this has been an incredible journey. I am grateful to one and all for the chance to live and work as I do. The thing is, I'm not done yet. Not even close.

CONTENTS

CHILDHOOD

(kinderdae)

DRAAI ROOMYS

I love soft serve ice cream. What kid doesn't? My thing with draai roomys began on beach holidays in Strand. They were such a treat, despite the mad queue outside N'Ice on a hot, sunny day. There were never enough paper serviettes, they melted too quickly, and someone in the gang inevitably dropped theirs and cried for another. Lekker.

The Afrikaans name comes from their appearance. Literally translated, 'draai roomys' means 'turn ice cream'. And since it comes out in a spiral, a boere kid would definitely ask pa for a draai roomys. To this day, I still love frozen treats. There's a secret stash of lollies in the freezer at home, and I always go for the frozen creation on the dessert menu. It's a weakness. I'm constantly fiddling with ideas for grown-up frozen desserts inspired by those summer treats from my childhood.

One of the ones I like best is an ice cream cone that mashes together a draai roomys, a King Cone and the boere tannie classic dessert – peppermint crisp tart. The latter is fridge tart with tinned caramel and Nestlé Peppermint Crisp that's so sweet it catches in your throat. There's a whole lot of nostalgia and heritage going on with every lick.

PEPPERMINT CRISP DELIGHT

2 tins Nestlé Caramel Treat (380g)
5 bars of Peppermint Crisp (49g)
2 cups cream
1 vanilla pod, scraped
8 sugar cones
8 sheets baking paper, roughly A5 size

Place 1 tin of Caramel Treat in a bowl and paddle with a spatula until the caramel is smooth. Grate three of the Peppermint Crisp bars on a fine grater and break the other two bars into large chunks for garnish later.

With your mixer (we love our Kitchenaid), whisk the cream and vanilla seeds until firm. Fold the cream into the softened Caramel Treat and fold though the grated Peppermint Crisp. Set the mixture aside.

Wrap the sugar cones in the paper to form a collar that protrudes roughly 5 cm above the cone. Secure it with tape. Place the other tin of Caramel Treat in a piping bag and pipe some into the bottom of each cone. Fill the cones with the Peppermint Crisp mixture so it sticks up above the cone. Place standing up in the freezer, preferably overnight. (We cut holes in upturned old ice cream containers to hold them.)

When you are ready to serve, remove the collars and garnish with the Peppermint Crisp chunks. I've also served them with more whipped cream and Caramel Popcorn.

Serves 4 to 6

KOS KOS SALAD

South Africa loves tinned pilchards. We consume truckloads of the stuff. Certain brands, like Lucky Star that are so iconic, feature in local pop art. There isn't a trading store or spaza shop in the country, no matter how remote, where you can't buy a tin of pilchards.

One tin is easily enough protein for three people. It's affordable, has a very long shelf-life, and travels well. A couple of tins in a rucksack can keep you going for a week. You don't even need to heat it, as the oily little fish can be eaten straight out of the tin. South Africans consume tens of thousands of cans of pilchards daily.

Tinned pilchards come in different flavours, but my favourite is the bog-standard pilchards in tomato sauce. We grew up with two staples made from tinned pilchards: fish cakes – the best with mash and peas – and a family favourite for a lazy Sunday dinner called Kos Kos. No one in the family knows where the name Kos Kos came from, but my mother grew up with it as a child. It's like a poor man's Niçoise, with ingredients from the corner shop – some chopped onions, tomato, cucumber, lettuce, mayo, hard-boiled eggs and tomato pilchards mixed together and eaten as a salad or on a sandwich. If you don't feel like cooking – Kos Kos!

It's definitely a family thing, because my aunty would make it when we went round there too. We loved it. I still make it for an easy supper at home. Of course, I use better ingredients now. My Ma couldn't get cos lettuce, and the mayo was off the shelf but the star of the dish is still pilchards in tomato sauce.

We are the third generation of Bassons – that we are aware of – that makes Kos Kos. I've sort of built on it by adding mayonnaise I make myself and caper berries.

2 heads cos lettuce, ripped
¼ large cucumber, sliced
1 avocado, diced
2 tomatoes, sliced
1 red onion, sliced
1 tin pilchards in
   tomato sauce (400g)
4 eggs, soft boiled
200 ml fresh mayonnaise
80 g caper berries

Starting with the lettuce, layer the cucumber, avo, tomato and onion in a large platter or bowl. Top with chunks of pilchards, soft boiled eggs broken in half, mayo and finally the caper berries. Serve with toasted sour dough.

Serves 4 to 6

PICKLED SARDINES

My ouma and oupa were like a pair of boere hippies. The more they could forage from the sea or their environment, the happier they were. The life they led was simple and full of joy.

They also took a tremendous delight in the old ways of growing and preserving their own food. They would tootle about in their old Land Rover, heading for a favourite fishing spot on the West Coast. In them, I think I caught a glimpse of who I would grow up to be. Of course one of their greatest shared joys was food.

I cherish some early childhood memories of eating all sorts of sea creatures at the table in their Malmesbury home. Fishing together was their thing. Ouma was the queen of galjoen fishing, and anything else she could gather: snoek, harders, mussels and crayfish came to the table cooked in a very simple way.

Pickled fish was served with fresh bread and jam, either as a starter or light meal. Jars and jars of it filled the pantry along with preserves, jams, cookies and rusks. Usually made with white fish like hake, it's a traditional Easter dish in the Cape, but I just love preparing it in our restaurants because it reminds me so much of my time with them.

PICKLING LIQUID

3 medium onions, sliced
1 clove garlic, crushed
20 g fresh ginger, sliced
1 fresh red chilli, split in half
125 ml vegetable oil
pinch of salt
1 tbsp good-quality
   curry powder
2 tsp turmeric
1 tsp cayenne pepper
2 bay leaves
5 cardamom pods
4 star anise
2 cinnamon sticks
¾ cup sugar
400 ml vinegar
700 ml water
3 carrots, sliced
2 tbsp corn flour

SARDINES

1 kg fresh sardines
250 g cake flour
1.5 L vegetable oil for deep frying

PICKLING LIQUID
Over a medium heat, in a large pot, salt and sweat off the onions, garlic, ginger and chilli in the oil for about 15 minutes. Add all the spices and sweat for a further 5 minutes. Next, add the sugar, vinegar and water to simmer slowly with the lid off for 45 minutes. (You can cook the sardines while this reduces.)

When you sardines are ready in their dish, add the thinly sliced carrots to the pickling liquid. Mix the corn flour into a paste with a little water and stir into the slow simmering liquid. Cook for approximately 5 minutes.

SARDINES
Your sardines should be cleaned, gutted and have the heads removed. Dust them well with the cake flour. Fry in the pre-heated oil at 180°C for approximately 4 minutes. Drain and place in a dish.

Pour the hot, bubbling pickling liquid over the sardines and leave to cool. This is best eaten at least one day after pickling, and will keep in the fridge for a week. (For texture, we serve it with deep-fried slivers of garlic.)

Serves 4 to 6

SNOEK

My dad braais a mean snoek. He's famous for it. We used to come down from Nelspruit to Yzerfontein on the West Coast on family holidays, and he would buy fresh snoek from the fishing boats and braai every day if he could. Six or eight of them would end up in the deep freeze and then he'd wrap them in newspaper for the drive back home.

Somehow, they'd always last the journey still frozen, and go into our own freezer for special occasions. Newspaper is the boere cooler box. The snoek provided us with a memory of our Cape holiday through out the year, and made us long for the next visit.

Braaied snoek was something I loved. There would be banter around the fire while he cooked, memories of the coast or regular family stuff about who was doing what; with the smell of the fire and all the opinions about the best way to keep it going, running back to the kitchen for this or that.

Finally, the perfectly cooked snoek would be laid out in the middle of the table for everyone to help themselves. For me it's a very communal meal. You all eat from this big fish, chatting and catching up on the day as you do. My favourite part is the backbone, charred from the fire and delicious. My brother and I always used to fight over it.

It was only later as a chef that I learned of the fish's broader significance. Snoek is poor man's food. It is said that it feeds the Western Cape. I've heard figures like 80 000 a day, but there's probably some research needed to find out exactly how many. For a very reasonable price, one fish can feed a whole family. It's extremely versatile too. You can braai, salt, smoke or stew it in a local dish called smoor snoek. Then there's the roe known as kuite, which are a local treat.

It is by no means easy to cook. Snoek is a challenging fish. They have a reputation for biting off fishermen's fingers, it goes soft very quickly, and has to be handled carefully. It is ugly and bony – but cooked correctly, it will blow your socks off.

SNOEK WITH APRICOT GLAZE

SNOEK
1 snoek, approximately 1.5 kg,
    flecked
handful coarse salt

GLAZE
100 g butter, soft
100 g apricot jam
1 lemon, juice and zest

GARNISH
crushed roasted almonds
dried apricots

Make a nice hot fire. Snoek is grilled over high heat. You need a folding or 'clapper' grid for this so it is easy to turn – snoek is oily and sticks terribly to a flat grid.

To 'fleck' or 'vlek' a snoek is to gut and clean it. Because of its unique anatomy, it's a particular skill among fishermen. Take it from me, leave it to someone who knows how.

Sprinkle coarse salt on both sides of the snoek, leave it to cure for 20 minutes, then wipe off the excess salt and pat it dry with a cloth or paper towel. Place it in your braai grid and hang it somewhere to air dry for another 20 minutes.

While the snoek is hanging in the breeze, mix the butter, apricot jam, lemon juice and zest together.

Place the snoek over hot coals, skin side first, for 2–3 minutes, being careful not to burn the skin. While it's cooking, baste the flesh side with the glaze. Turn the snoek over, the butter dripping into the fire will create flame and smoke. Don't stress, it is part of the process!

Leave the snoek on the flesh side until it is beautifully caramelised. This should take about 3–4 minutes. Fish cooks quickly, so don't wander off.

Carefully remove the snoek from the grid, dress with crushed roasted almonds and dried apricots and serve.

Serves 4 to 6

MIA SE PAMPOENTERT (PUMPKIN PIE)

This cooking thing really runs in the family. My first ever job as a chef was at the Royal Hotel in Riebeek Casteel in 1997. It just so happened that my cousin, Mia, had worked there a couple of years before me, and left quite a legacy behind her.

In my view, Mia cooks traditional South African food far, far better than I do. It's in her bones. She still lives in our oupa and ouma's house in Malmesbury and runs a baking shop in the town. When I arrived at the Royal, the shiniest part of her legacy there was her pumpkin tart. I was taught to cook 'Mia se Pampoentert' by the ladies who worked in the kitchen. Most of them were illiterate, so nothing was written down, but they knew it by heart as it was a popular standard in the restaurant.

As I do with recipes I like, I dragged it with me wherever I went. It is a testament both to the quality of the dish and to Mia's skill as a cook that I have never fiddled with the core recipe. We serve it sometimes at Overture as a side service to our main courses. The only change is that we add a pumpkin seed granola for texture. It's partly about showing off the fact that we love eating sweet sides with our savoury meals. It's also about serving an amazing dish steeped in my heritage as a cook and a South African.

At Spice Route, we use the same recipe, but serve it with caramel mousse and chocolate ice cream for dessert. It really is such an amazing and flexible recipe. It appears here unchanged, and true. A testament to Mia's ability as a cook, and the fact that the love for food runs deep in our blood.

125 g melted butter
¾ cup sugar
4 eggs
½ cup cake flour
1 tbsp baking powder
250 ml milk
500 ml cooked butternut
cinnamon to dust
castor sugar to dust

Preheat the oven to 180°C.

Cream together the butter and sugar. Add the eggs one at a time, beating after each addition.

Now sieve flour and baking powder together, and add it to the mixture, mixing until everything is incorporated.
This should be followed by the milk. As you pour it steadily in, whisk continuously to ensure a smooth batter.

The butternut you use should be ripe. We cube and cook it so it is soft, but not a slush. Add the cooked butternut to the mixture and combine well.

Scoop into an oven-proof dish and lightly dust with cinnamon and castor sugar.

Bake for 20 minutes until firm and golden.

Serves 4 to 6

TONGUE

Marrying Mareli Botha opened up a whole new world of food to me. Of course we were united by our shared love for food, but there's a deeper connection. Most married guys I know make a thing of complaining about their in-laws coming round. For me it's a total adventure in food.

Ma Benita and Pa Johan love a good meal and a wyntjie, which is fantastic, but they also bring their own unique food heritage to the table. It seems a bit old hat to repeat that I always look to my own heritage and family recipes for the inspiration for my own ideas. Mareli and her family brought a whole ocean of undiscovered ideas through the front door with them.

There's an adaptation of one of Mareli's mom's standard recipes on the menu at Spice Route. We took her delicious and very traditional soet mostert tong with white rice, deconstructed it a little to make it prettier, and it's been a popular item on the menu since day one.

You know those cookbooks from the 1970s with bad photos and recipes you think you would never cook, let alone eat? Those are part of this country's heritage. They are how we got to cooking like we do, and why we yearn for certain comfort foods. My food inspiration comes from everywhere. It comes from those old books, but it also comes from people around me who carry those old standards forward and continue to make them a feature of our cultural landscape.

Ma Benita's recipe was passed down from Ouma Jossie, her late mother-in-law. She turned it into a staple of her repertoire for entertaining. I had it on a visit to them before our wedding, and loved it so much that I ripped it off. She was very understanding and even offered input on the final menu dish, which included baby onions pickled in a mustard sauce. It just proves again how good food and recipes can transcend generations.

SWEET MUSTARD TONGUE

1 pickled, cooked tongue
   (350–400 g)

SAUCE
225 ml water
3 egg yolks
4 tsp mustard powder
   (Colmans is best)
110 ml white wine vinegar
½ cup sugar
1 tbsp corn flour
1 tsp salt

ASSEMBLY
5 baby onions
8–12 baby heirloom beetroot
100 g feta cheese
bunch parsley, snipped
   or micro greens

These days you can actually buy cooked tongue, but you can easily cook your own by simmering it in salted water.

To make the mustard sauce, combine all those ingredients in a heavy saucepan. Whisk vigorously over medium heat until the sauce thickens. Remove from the heat and cool. Peel the baby onions, cut in half and cook in salted boiling water until tender. Mix the soft baby onions into the mustard sauce

Simmer the beetroot in salted water until soft and then cool them in their cooking water. Peel and then quarter or thinly slice them. We alternate so you get the different colours and textures in the dish.

Preheat your oven to 220°C. Slice the tongue into 2–3 mm slices. Lay them flat in an oven-proof baking dish and cover with the mustard sauce mixture. Crumble the feta over and bake for 15 minutes to heat the tongue through and caramelise the feta and sauce. Dress with finely chopped parsley and beetroot.

Serves 6

CABBAGE

Cabbage is a part of my food heritage in a way that is common to most kids: I wouldn't eat cabbage when I was a kid. In fact, my mom got a proper run-around from me at almost every mealtime.

Most people complain about the smell of cooking cabbage or a horrible experience with cabbage at boarding school. Cabbage and the brassica family seem to get the worst stick from kids. They feature in the tear-jerking stories of grown-ups long after the damage is done. None of that for me. If it was good for you, I would not be having it, period.

My Afrikaans Ma was resourceful though, and found a way to get me to eat cabbage. I love the stuff today. If a kid in a boere home won't eat his veggies, the go-to strategy after threats and pleas is to bury that shit in cheese. A bechamel sauce and a grilled cheese topping can do a lot to get the greens in. So that's where cabbage gratin came onto play in my childhood home, and it is a memory that has stuck with me. We use it as the base for a side dish from time to time, usually with the addition of ham or bacon.

Global food trends have brought us new varieties of cabbage for moms to carry into battle with their kids. There's Savoy, red, Chinese, even variations on their cousins like kale and Brussels sprouts. I love them all thanks to my mom and cabbage gratin. To think I might have missed out on ribs and slaw, buttered Brussel's sprouts with salt and pepper; and what would chakalaka be without finely sliced green cabbage?

Today, we buy our cabbages from the Epping Market in Cape Town by the bagful. In South Africa cabbage forms the backbone of quite a few traditional dishes, and they are sold in bags of 8. It still takes me back to my mother's table.

CABBAGE & HAM BAKE

half a cabbage

SAUCE
650 ml milk
2 cloves garlic
2 tsp salt
2 peppercorns
1 generous grating nutmeg
1 sprig fresh thyme
80 g butter
80 g flour
150 g mature cheddar
1 tbsp Dijon mustard
1 tbsp wholegrain mustard

300 g cooked ham, diced
100 g mature cheddar
**   for topping**

Preheat the oven to 180°C.

Rip the cabbage into chunks and bring a large pot of salted water to the boil. Cook until soft (roughly 15 minutes) then refresh in iced water and drain well, patting dry with a cloth.

In a medium pot combine the milk, garlic, salt, peppercorns, nutmeg and thyme. Bring to the boil then turn off the heat and leave it to infuse for 20 minutes, then strain through a fine sieve.

Make a roux by melting the butter over medium heat in a saucepan. When the butter comes to an even bubble, stir in the flour to form a smooth paste. Slowly whisk in the warm, infused milk, whisking until the sauce thickens and comes to a boil. Turn down the heat and cook slowly, while stirring, for 10 minutes.

Take the pot off the heat, whisk in the cheese allocated to the sauce and stir in the mustard to combine well.

Mix the cooked cabbage, sauce and ham together and transfer to an ovenproof dish. Check seasoning then sprinkle the rest of the cheese on top. Bake at 180°C for 30 minutes.

Serves 4 to 6

HOME-GROUND SAMP PAP & BUTTER ROASTED CAULIFLOWER

When we lived in Nelspruit, there was a Zulu woman named Lena who worked for my family as a housekeeper. My mother baked for a home industry in Nelspruit, and as the orders mounted, she trained Lena to help her. The two of them worked really hard to build that business.

Although the landscape is changing, many middle-class South Africans grew up having their domestic cleaning, laundry and child-care needs and even daily cooking taken care of by 'the maid'. Lena provided this layered care for our home before her status changed with the baking business.

She was a bird-like, skinny woman with huge spectacles who would stand no nonsense from us kids. On weekday afternoons when we got home from school, Lena would share her pot of pap with us. This is a staple of southern Africa. Known variously as pap, puthu, mealie-meal, sadza and a variety of names from region to region, it is essentially a stiff porridge made from maize meal.

Just as Italians have polenta, so South Africans have pap. It might be eaten for breakfast as a soft porridge, or as a meal on its own. It is served as a firm porridge with a wild spinach stew, braised or braaied meat, usually with a spicy tomato sauce. It is also cooked as a steamed pap, which is crumbly and nutty. We call it krummel pap, and the best part is where it caramelises at the bottom of the pot like the crust of a paella. There was nothing like Lena's pap pot after school.

Whenever I eat pap, or cook a new version of this staple, Lena comes to mind. Lena and that pap pot.

250 g whole samp
1 large cauliflower
1 tsp salt
100 g butter, cubed
1 L water (for cooking)
150 ml amasi
1 lemon, zest and juice
1 tsp thyme, freshly picked

Grind the samp coarsely in a blender. Cover with cold water and leave in the fridge to soak overnight.

Pre-heat your oven to 180°C.

Place the cauliflower in a baking dish, stalks, leaves and all. Season with the salt and dot with butter. Roast in the oven, basting continuously with melted butter, until the head is tender (about 45 minutes).

Bring the litre of water to a boil in a pot with a pinch of salt. Stir in the samp with the water it was soaked in. Cook out the samp, while whisking, at a low temperature for 15–20 minutes. It should become rich and creamy.

Whisk in the amasi and add the lemon juice. Correct the seasoning with salt and pour the rich samp into your serving dish. Place the cauliflower on top of the samp. Dress with some butter from the roasting dish, picked thyme and lemon zest.

FRIKKADELS

This is probably the story of thousands of South African homes; the love of the frikkadel. Not only do people love them for texture and flavour, they provide an affordable meal that's relatively easy to make. For those who didn't grow up with it, frikkadels are a sort of cross between a meatball and meatloaf.

There were three kinds made in our house when I was growing up. There was a plain one, a curry one and a tomato one. The curry, or kerrie, frikkadels was made with an iconic off-the-shelf curry powder called Maharajah. It would make the mixture bright yellow because of the turmeric in it, but it was fantastic. As we got older, my ma would experiment with hotter and hotter variants, and the meatballs got redder and redder from the chilli powder.

The base was mincemeat, usually the cheapest thing down at the butcher. From 500 g or 600 g you could feed a family of four comfortably. But if there was a kilo of mince in the mix that was school sandwiches for a couple of days too.

My Ma would make her tamatie frikkadels a day in advance and leave in the fridge overnight. They were like a self-marinating ball of goodness, my favourite one of all. It has a very specific flavour profile connected to our Dutch roots, and it's a comfort food like mac and cheese, or spaghetti and meatballs. I would say that this was the basis of my all-time favourite family meal.

Frikkadels have appeared on menus in many incarnations in my career. Using Ma's basic recipe as a base, I've done them with mushrooms from the forest near Overture, or in a sort of upscale puttanesca version. The one with pasture-reared beef and mushrooms has been an enduring favourite of mine though.

TAMATIE FRIKKADELS

FRIKKADELS
knob of butter
1 large onion, finely chopped
2 cloves garlic, finely chopped
250 g streaky bacon, diced
250 g mushrooms, sliced
200 g sour dough bread
200 ml milk
1 tbsp salt
2 eggs
1 kg beef mince
small handful chopped parsley

TOMATO SAUCE
8 tomatoes, diced
30 g basil, ripped
2 garlic cloves, sliced
1 bunch spring onions, sliced
100 ml olive oil
30 ml Balsamic vinegar
salt and pepper to taste
75 g Parmesan, grated
75 g breadcrumbs
Parmesan to garnish

Preheat the oven to 180°C.

Heat a large skillet and add the knob of butter. Wait for the butter to turn slightly brown, then sauté the onions, garlic, bacon and mushrooms until they are nicely caramelised. Remove from heat, transfer to a bowl and leave to cool.

Tear the bread into chunks and soak in the milk for 10 minutes. Combine with the salt, eggs, mince and parsley, and mix thoroughly with your hands. Add the cooled onion mixture and work it into the mince well. You want an even distribution of all the ingredients.

Roll the mixture into 8 balls of roughly 125 g each and set aside. You don't have to be too acurate about it – we weigh stuff off for portion control in the restaurant. Just note, though, that if you make them too big, the frikkadels won't cook through.

For the sauce, mix the tomatoes, basil, garlic, spring onions, olive oil and balsamic vinegar together and season. Spoon this mixture into a baking dish and place the frikkadels on top.

Cover with the Parmesan and bread crumbs, then bake the dish for approximately 40 minutes.

Sprinkle with some more Parmesan before serving.

Serves 6 to 8

MONKEY GLAND SAUCE

There's this thing about me that people in the restaurant and food media industry find very strange. I love Spur. I flippin' love it. I regularly sneak off to my local Spur for a mid-week dinner. But my favourite is when I've been travelling and I get to a local airport and they have a Spur. I get straight in there for a monkey gland burger. For me it is such a taste of home.

I grew up in the Spur. Since 1967, Spur has been known as the official restaurant of the South African family. That was definitely true for my family. We did birthday parties and special occasions, sure, but actually we'd find any excuse to head down to Spur for a meal. For me, Spur has helped create countless special memories in that sort of special, value-for-money, chain steakhouse way.

Its popularity may have declined over time and with so many other options in the market, but I still love popping into a Spur. People look down their noses at the franchise, but I believe that many of our collective food memories are somehow wrapped up in that strange Native American-themed chain of steakhouses.

Whether they care to admit it or not, everyone has their particular favourite Spur menu item. For some it's the ribs, or the onion rings, or those hot rock steaks they secretly crave. For me, it's the monkey gland burger.

30 ml vegetable oil

2 medium onions,
    finely chopped

2 cloves garlic, crushed

2 tsp thyme

1 tbsp cayenne pepper

100 ml chutney

75 ml Worcestershire sauce

30 ml vinegar

150 ml water

60 ml sugar

500 ml All Gold
    tomato sauce

In a little oil, sweat the onion over a medium heat with the garlic, thyme and cayenne pepper. Don't brown the onions, take your time. You want them translucent, with the aromatics nicely infused – approximately 15 minutes.

Add the rest of the ingredients and bring to a gentle simmer. The idea is to reduce the volume by one third, being careful not to burn the sauce. It must at least be of coating consistency – it should coat the back of a spoon dipped into it.

When you are happy with the consistency, blend the sauce and pass it through a fine sieve. Serve as a sauce, or use the glaze to baste steaks, chicken or ribs.

Makes 1 litre

MELK TERT

We do tea and cake very well in South Africa. This deeply entrenched cultural habit probably has its roots somewhere in the English high tea, but the boere tannies decided that the perfect time for a tea party is in the morning.

I remember attending a lot of these with my mother before I went to school. It was hellishly competitive. Each of the ladies would try to put on the best spread, trying to one-up the other tannies in the group. Milk tart often formed the centre of the sweet and savoury offering, and it was hotly contested territory.

Our generation seems to have dropped the tradition completely. We meet in coffee shops and eat bacon croissants with fancy blends. My mother and her friends still do 'koek en tee' on a Monday after their bible study meeting though.

I reckon the melk tert is the crown princess of the 'koek en tee' circuit. Its origin is uncertain – it could derive from the English custard tart, Portuguese pasteis de nata, or a wide selection of baked European custards. The tannies have made it their own though, and it is firmly established as an iconic Afrikaans treat.

We produce two different milk tarts in South Africa. One has a hot, thickened milk mixture that is poured into a pre-baked sweet pastry shell. The other is a custard that is lightened up with whipped egg white and baked in a raw flaky pastry shell. In the oven, the mixture will soufflé because of moisture and aerated egg whites. It falls back into its shell as the tart cools down.

The latter version has inspired one of my favourite deserts, the milk tart soufflé. We started serving it at Overture, and it has stuck. I like this bit of cultural appropriation as a way to take the milk tart with me on my restaurant journey.

If you want to make this, be warned – like the tannies at bible study meetings, you have to put in the effort. The only way to bake good soufflés is by practising a lot. Maybe you can start a melk tert soufflé tradition at book club or something. A bit of competition will do wonders for your baking.

Note that in the recipe I've created based on my memory of a melk tert, we make two different custards and combine them to make the soufflé. The first one is a classic soufflé base, and the other is a family recipe for milk tart which I've adapted. Putting them together creates a dessert that will rise well and still have that classic melk tert flavour.

MILK TART SOUFFLÉ

CRÈME PATISSERIE BASE
125 ml milk
2 egg yolks
2 tbsp castor sugar
2½ tsp corn flour

MILK TART BASE
125 ml milk
rind of 1 lemon
1 tbsp white sugar
1 tsp ground cinnamon
1 egg
1 tbsp cake flour
1 tsp corn flour
pinch of salt
1 tsp butter

100 g castor sugar
100 g soft butter

250 g egg whites (8 eggs)
¾ cup castor sugar

Make the crème patisserie base by bringing the milk to a boil. In a bowl, cream the yolks, castor sugar and corn flour until the mixture is white and airy. Now pour the hot milk over the egg mixture and whisk thoroughly. Strain the mixture back into a pot and whisk constantly over medium heat until thick. Pour into a container and set aside to cool.

For the milk tart base, in a saucepan, gently bring the milk with lemon rind, sugar and ground cinnamon to a simmer over a medium heat. Cream the egg, cake flour, corn flour and salt together until white and airy. Strain the milk mixture and melt the butter into the milk. Pour hot milk over the egg mixture and whisk through. Put the mixture back on the stove over medium heat and stir constantly until thick. Pour into a container and set aside to cool. Cool both the bases down with a layer of plastic wrap pushed onto it, to prevent a skin forming.

Brush your soufflé moulds – you can use 4 large ramekins or ovenproof coffee mugs of 250 ml capacity – with a thin layer of soft butter. Refrigerate until the butter hardens.

Now brush your soufflé moulds with a thin layer of soft butter again and coat with a thin layer of castor sugar. Return the moulds to the fridge.

Preheat your oven to 175°C.

Combine the two cooled custard bases in a large bowl and whisk together until smooth. Start whisking the egg whites in a mixer until soft peaks form. Add the castor sugar slowly and whisk at high speed until a firm, smooth meringue has formed. Be careful not to over-whisk the meringue to a dry stage.

Now whisk a third of the meringue into the base mixture. Fold in the balance of the meringue gently with a spatula. Immediately scoop into the prepared moulds, being careful not to mess on the sides. I like to leave the top of the soufflé quite rough, as it gives this majestic light dessert a homey feel.

Tap the ramekins or moulds to remove any air pockets. If any of the mixture spills onto the rim, clean it off. Bake immediately for 8–10 minutes until well-risen and golden brown.

Dust with a mixture of icing sugar and ground cinnamon and serve straight from the oven.

Serves 4

TANNIE HETTA

My Ma, Tannie Hetta, is one of three sisters who all cook like a dream. I'm sure everyone thinks their mom is the best cook, but mine really is. It's because of her, and the family traditions of cooking and baking that she channelled into my childhood, that I am the chef I am today.

There are lots of things that I have taken or adapted from her kitchen over time. There are echoes of her cooking in my restaurants and in my cooking style. It's in my nature to fiddle and push boundaries with recipes, so sometimes they aren't recognisable as Ma's, but there is one glorious recipe from my childhood that I have reproduced absolutely faithfully. Ma's apple tart is the Holy Grail.

I use it over and over. It became a bit of a sensation on season 1 of the Ultimate Braaimaster. Somehow it has become a symbol of how my personal and national heritage have come to influence my cooking and menus so strongly. To acknowledge this and my Ma's contribution to my career, we printed the recipe on tea towels for Spice Route.

Ma is a mean baker, as suggested by the home industry baking business she ran with Lena. She took a traditional apple tart and turned it into a masterpiece by poaching the apples and baking them in a sponge cake batter. It's somewhat different from the normal South African tart, but it is a wonderful evolution.

She sometimes call's it a Greek apple tart, but although the idea for poaching the fruit comes from there, soaking it with delicious sugary syrup is pure boerevrou.

What makes it so perfect is that it is equally delicious eaten hot, straight out of the oven, or left-over, cold and crunchy from the fridge. All that sugar syrup crystallises on the top. Of course, it has to survive the night and a ravenous family to morph into the cold crunchy state, so it's often best to make two.

The only permissible variation lies in what it is served with. In our home, it was homemade custard and vanilla ice cream. Around these parts we innovate with almond ice cream or a cinnamon crème Anglaise or something else that lets us claim back some ownership from the master baker in the family.

TANNIE HETTA'S APPLE TART

4 large green apples

750ml water
250ml white wine
150g sugar
1 cinnamon stick
2 cardamom pods, crushed
2 star anise

3 eggs
70g milk
60g butter
140g sugar
130g flour
10g baking powder
pinch of salt

250g cream
250g sugar
1 vanilla pod, scraped

Preheat you oven to 180°C. Peel, core and quarter the apples.

In a pot, bring the water, wine, sugar, cinnamon, cardamom and start anise to the boil. Add the apples and weigh them down with a saucer so they remain immersed in the syrup while they poach for 15 minutes.

As a word of caution, some apples cook faster than others, so be careful not to overcook. Remove them from the heat and leave to cool and infuse in the poaching syrup.

Whisk the eggs and milk together. Cream the butter and sugar together until pale. Sift the dry ingredients together into a bowl. Now beat in a bit of egg mixture, then some butter mixture, then more egg, alternating between the two. Beat between each addition until it is all combined.

Pour the resulting smooth batter into your baking tin. Lay the cooled apples on top and push them into the batter. Bake at 180°C, until golden brown (about 30 minutes).

While the apple tart is in the oven, combine the cream, sugar and vanilla seeds in a small saucepan. Simmer until all the sugar is dissolved. Pour the resulting hot syrup over the apple tart as it comes out of the oven.

Serve with cream, ice cream or custard.

Serves 4 to 6

ORANGE CAKE WITH RUM & RAISIN

Christmas at my grandparents' house was always supposed to be a very simple affair. It was all about family, and everybody was asked to bring a dish. But it always seemed to end up the biggest display of gammons, turkeys and other festive fare that you could imagine.

As a kid, that was not really so interesting to me. I really was a picky eater. But for every platter of Christmas food that came through the door, a dessert arrived too. There was everything. I couldn't wait to tear into the trifles, ice creams, meringues, roly-polys and boerejongens (which the kids were never allowed to eat because they were just about pure brandy).

Then there was Tannie Marisa's awesome rum & raisin concoction. I'm not sure where it came from, but it was her specialty. We were always allowed a bit, because rum wasn't really alcohol was it? I loved that flavour, and I still make her recipe. It's great on ice cream, pancakes, waffles, but the combination with orange cake is just the best. It reminds me of family and Christmas every time.

5 eggs
⅔ cup sugar
½ cup flour
2½ tsp baking powder
75 ml cream
100 g butter, melted
30 ml orange liqueur
1 vanilla pod, scraped
1 orange, zested and segmented

GARNISH
125 g raisins
80 g brown sugar
250 ml water
pinch of cinnamon
75 g butter
lashings of good, dark rum

Preheat the oven to 160°C.

Cream the eggs and sugar until light and fluffy. Sift the flour and baking powder into the egg mixture. Fold through the cream, melted butter and orange liqueur. Add the orange zest and vanilla seeds.

Grease 4 large ramekins and divide the batter equally among them.

Bake at 160°C for approximately 25 minutes. A skewer inserted into the centre of the cake should come out clean if it is cooked through, and it should be golden brown.

Combine the raisins, brown sugar, water, cinnamon and butter in a small saucepan and cook over medium heat. After approximately 15 minutes of simmering the sauce should become slightly thicker and glossy.

Add a generous lashing of rum and light to flambé.

Pour the flaming rum and raisin sauce over the orange cakes and garnish with orange segments.

Serves 6 to 8

HERTZOGGIES

Hertzoggies are these little sweet pastries that talk to the heart of what it means to grow up Afrikaans. There are named after General Hertzog, who was the prime minister of South Africa from 1924 to 1939. Apparently they were his favourite cookies, and they continue to be a firm community favourite at every kind of gathering from kerk bazaars to koek en tee with your aunty.

Hetrzoggies talk to tradition, heritage and history, remembering the past and respect for one's elders. The love of baking is in the case, the thrifty habit of making preserves is in the apricot jam filling, and the use of dried pantry goods features in the desiccated coconut meringue topping.

Our insatiable sweet tooth is present in every bite. All this cultural complexity is wrapped up in one delicious little tart.

Of course I grew up with Hertzoggies. My life would not be the same without Tannie Sanna's delicious cookies. There would be piles of them when we visited her in Riebeek Kasteel. She would bake them in tonnes to ensure that there were shit-loads to eat. Lucky that; it is almost impossible to eat just one. Even today, I can't walk past a tray of Hertzoggies at a flea market or fete without trying one. They are incredibly wrapped up in so many of my happy memories of childhood.

They're kind of a mix between a little tart and a cookie. There's a perfectly cool balance between the slight saltiness of the pastry and the sweetness of the apricot jam, finished off with the fantastic crunchy texture of the coconut.

Another thing that contributes to their iconic cultural status is that Hertzoggies preserve very well. Never mind the three-day car journey to visit family, you can make piles of them at the start of school holidays and still be enjoying them at Christmas. They are just fantastic.

HERTZOGGIE PAVLOVA

MERINGUE
250 g egg whites (8 eggs)
250 g granulated sugar
250 g icing sugar, sifted

CRÈME PATISSERIE
½ cup sugar
6 egg yolks
40 g flour
500 ml milk
1 vanilla pod, split and scraped

TOPPING
300 ml cream, whipped
   to firm peak
1 tin apricots in syrup
   (410 g), drained
175 g toasted coconut shavings

Whip the egg whites until soft peaks form. Slowly add the sugar until it is all incorporated and whisk into a firm peak meringue. Gently fold the icing sugar into the meringue. Pipe two equal disks onto silicone mats.

Bake in a pre-heated oven at 120°C for 90 minutes. Remove from the oven and allow to cool on the mats. The meringue should be crispy on the outside with a chewy centre.

Make the filling by creaming the egg yolks and sugar until light and fluffy. Sift in the flour and mix thoroughly. Bring the milk and scraped vanilla pod to the boil in a saucepan. As soon as it comes to the boil, pour the milk through a sieve directly into the egg-yolk mixture. Scrape this mixture back into the saucepan and whisk continuously over a moderate heat until the mixture comes to a light bubble and thickens up.

Pass the crème patisserie through a sieve again to ensure that it is 100% smooth. Cover with cling wrap, pushing it onto the crème patisserie to prevent a skin from forming. Refrigerate until cold.

Place the first disk of meringue on a serving dish. In a mixing bowl, whisk the créme patisserie until smooth, and fold in the whipped cream.

Dress the meringue, alternating blobs of crème patisserie with apricots and coconut shavings. Put the next meringue disk on top and repeat. We added soetkoekies on top for texture.

Serves 8 to 10

MY HOOD
(my mense)

BUTTERMILK SCONES

Scones are a delicious hangover from our days as part of the British Empire. Like our Sunday roasts, pies, steamed puddings and a host of other things, we've embroidered them into our lexicon. It's amazing how many boere tannies won't think of having people round without baking fresh scones.

There's a lady down the road from us in Jamestown who bakes scones for the neighbourhood. She's strict about when you collect them too. She needs to know exactly what time your guests will arrive so you can fetch them 5 minutes before. Her scones have to steam when people crack them open.

Just as vital as an oven-fresh scone is the preserves and other toppings you enjoy them with. I just love scones. I also love the way we eat them with fig jam and grated cheddar, or more like the English version with strawberry jam and whipped cream. That cream has to be sweet for the tannies, though. Clotted cream never made the cut here. I've even been served Orley whip on scones in South Africa.

Scones as we know them have a cousin in another pioneer society spawned by British colonisation. Across the Atlantic, the American biscuit referred to in "biscuits and gravy" is in fact a scone that is served with savoury dishes like braises and stews. In this, they are more like traditional local African dumplings called 'dombolo'. Those things are awesome. They are made with a yeast-based, bread-like dough and cooked on top of the stew like a sort of lid.

It is these that inspire the way we use a buttermilk scone recipe in the restaurant. They are like baked dumplings in a saucy dish. This simple, alternative application for the scone shows how diverse our cuisine can be.

240 g self-raising flour
30 g castor sugar
pinch of salt
1 tsp baking powder
60 g butter
250 ml buttermilk
milk for glazing

Sieve the flour, sugar, salt and baking powder together. Rub the butter into the dry ingredients until it has a light sandy texture.

Make a well in the centre of the mixture and add the buttermilk. Slowly stir the mixture, incorporating the flour gradually.

Press the dough together; being careful not to overwork it.

Divide into equal pieces and roll into small balls and place on top of your favourite casserole or stew. In this case we used saucy duck confit with young vegetables.

Glaze the scones with milk, and bake on for 20 minutes at 190°C.

Serves 4 to 6

BREAD

There's this on-going battle in the food world about gluten and all the ailments it gives rise to. The worst thing you could ever do to me would be to tell me I'm gluten intolerant. I love bread. In fact baked goods and me are like jam in a doughnut – messy to separate.

It is certainly true that the excessive consumption of heavily refined and modified flours cannot be good for you. It's tragic that some people are cursed with severe reactions to gluten, just tragic. However, I really think that, intolerant or not, you need to choose the source of the gluten carefully.

I have a friend named Fritz who owns a place in Stellenbosch called Schoon. He opened my eyes to a lot of sane perspectives about bread. In my opinion, we bake a pretty tidy loaf at Overture and Spice Route, but it has to be said that those breads don't hold a candle to Fritz's fare. For a start, he bakes his bread dark, just like a traditional old-world baker. He taught me that texture changes flavour, or influences it. The chew on a darker loaf changes how it tastes.

You can't just grab some flour and some packet yeast down at the supermarket and hope to make decent bread. It's all about ingredients and technique. Almost all bread has the same ingredients: flour, yeast, salt and water. The variable in all bread are the quantity of these ingredients and the mixing time.

To make bread is simple, but I have come to realise that the simpler food is, the harder it is to make well. True greatness only comes from doing simple things right, over and over. Kids at cooking school might be given a recipe from which they can produce bread. To be able to produce great bread from that recipe, they have to bake it a thousand times or more. Only if you wake up in the early hours for the baking shift over and over, learning about the subtle interplay between ingredients, moisture, time and temperature can you field a truly great loaf. Fritz has that knowledge.

We go to Schoon at least once a week for breakfast and to buy bread for home. To help Fritz out, I usually get a few pasteis de nata from the pasty case to see if the quality is declining. (Not because I'm addicted, but to help a friend.)

It is in conversation with him that our ciabatta started to take its current shape. What I learned from Fritz could fill a book, but it is illustrated nicely in a recipe that doesn't require fermenting and allows a novice to produce an acceptable loaf. Remember, practice makes perfect. Technique is what makes the bread, not the recipe.

CORIANDER SEED CIABATTA

700 g white bread flour
300 g cake flour
40 g salt
55 g sugar
2 tsp coriander seeds
40 g fresh yeast
300 g sour dough
800 g water

Roast, and then crush the coriander seeds with pestle and mortar. Place the flours, salt, sugar, coriander seeds, yeast and sour dough into a standmixer bowl and add water. Mix at a low speed for all the ingredients to incorporate then change to a high speed for approximately 10 minutes until elastic.

Note* Use a k-beater or dough paddle and not a dough hook.

Place the dough into a floured bowl and cover with plastic. Place in a warm area to prove until doubled in size, approximately 60–90 minutes.

Flour your surface and gently place your dough onto the table, being very careful not to knock out any air. Using a dough cutter, cut away at the dough and portion into 4 loaves and lightly shape by tucking the sides in.

Place on a sprayed and floured tray.

Bake at 250°C until a crust has formed – approximately 12 minutes – then drop temperature to 180°C for approximately 20 minutes.

Remove from the oven and cool on a wire rack.

Note* When shaping, be careful not to over work the dough to avoid losing the air in the dough. Because we don't do a second proving, we rely on keeping as much air in the dough as possible.

We us the same dough for vetkoek, we just cut it and drop it straight into a fryer. This technique of cutting vetkoek after proving was learnt from an old lady in Khayamandi. Fry until golden brown.

Makes 4 loaves

GATSBY

A trip to the Epping Municipal Market for ingredients for the restaurant is one of my absolute favourite outings. Ever since we started shopping for our vegetable staples at the market, I try not to miss a trip. It's a hell of an early start, but worth it.

I don't go for the shopping though. Who wants to be haggling with farmers in a warehouse full of produce at 6 in the morning? I go because we always hit Golden Dish for a Gatsby afterwards, a great bonding moment with my crew.

The Gatsby, like its counterpart the bunny chow in Durban, is a creation designed to feed the working class punter cheaply and with maximum flavour. A few places claim to have invented it, but my favourite is the one from Golden Dish. It's an absolute institution in the area, and it was certainly the site of my first experience of a Gatsby. Those things are the best hangover food on the planet, but my first Gatsby experience wasn't after a boozy evening out.

After a morning at the Epping Market with my good friend Alistaire Lawrence, he decided to take me on a tour of Athlone. This vibrant suburb of Cape Town is his 'hood and he wanted to show me the sights. After visiting a few of his old haunts like the legendary Galaxy Night Club, we needed a bite. Right near Galaxy, and probably the last stop on the way home for many party animals, stands Golden Dish. Guided by Alistaire, I ordered a half-Gatsby with masala steak, egg and cheese. It came with a range of sweet and spicy sauces, and a helping of vinegar chips.

Gatsby is shared food. You can stick anything you want in a Gatsby, but my favourite is masala steak, particularly the one at Golden Dish in Athlone. My dream Gatsby has got the following things happening in it: fresh tomato, shredded lettuce, yellow cheese, mustard mayo, fried eggs and slap chips (with brown vinegar).

GOURMAY GATSBY

Like any recipe, you can add the best ingredients – or the worst – and the result will be entirely dependent on those. In the spirit of its original creation from odds and ends in the kitchen I'll leave the choice of trimmings and bread to you.

This is my recipe for making the masala steak. Even the masala is up to you. Ask at the spice shop what they think will go best with steak, as each has their own recipe. The key to this is experimentation.

4 tbsp masala
2 cloves of crushed garlic
2 tsp salt
50 g sugar
2 sirloin steaks (200 g each)
dash of oil

Mix the masala, garlic, salt and sugar together. Rub the resulting paste into the steaks, making sure they are evenly coated. Cover the meat in a bowl and leave overnight in the fridge to marinate. It needs at least six hours to get the flavours nicely absorbed.

Before cooking, say an hour before, take the steaks out of the fridge and allow them to get up to room temperature. Grill or braai the meat to your liking. I like mine medium rare for a Gatsby; if they're too rare, they add to the mess of eating one.

Once cooked and well rested, slice the steak across the grain very thinly. It breaks up better if sliced across the grain, and you want lots of nice thin slices so the masala steak flavour is well distributed through the Gatsby.

Stick it into the Gatsby with your favourite ingredients. I really like a sharp cheddar and a fruity chutney with masala steak. You can shred in lettuce and add tomato and pickles. I've even put slap chips in one!

PERI-PERI

Nelspruit is home to a large and active Portuguese community. While I was growing up there, I couldn't avoid exposure to Portuguese cooking and flavours. It seemed everyone ate slap chips with peri-peri. I know I talk about all the things that come to me from my Afrikaans heritage, but South African heritage has a lot of that as well as a big pot of indigenous cultural flavours, including English, German and Portuguese.

I still love peri-peri and will eat it on just about everything. Funny thing is, Mareli also loves peri-peri. She also grew up in Nelspruit; in fact her folks still live there. We grew up there, went to the same schools, attended the same church but we never met because we were three years apart in age. One of the first things we discovered about each other's childhood there when we went back together, was that we loved peri-peri slap chips.

While I was working in Cape Town and abroad, and Mareli was studying in Stellenbosch, a new player in the Portuguese fast food game came to prominence in Nelspruit. We were both introduced separately to Tannie Soa's yellow caravan of Portuguese delights. Now, whenever we go visit, we eat at the caravan at least twice.

Her peri-peri everything is fantastic. If Mareli's mom comes to visit, she brings some of the sauce from the yellow caravan. There are always a couple of half-finished bottles in the fridge. Here's my version with a big bow to Tannie Sao.

PERI-PERI CHICKEN

SAUCE
20 g dried red chillies
100 g fresh red chillies
5 cloves garlic, finely chopped
5 tbsp sugar
2 tbsp salt
a fist full of fresh coriander
4 lemons, zested and juiced
250 ml spirit vinegar
1 tsp cayenne pepper
2 tsp paprika
1 tsp whole coriander seeds
1 tsp whole cumin

2 free-range chickens

Put everything except the chicken in your blender. Blitz it into a chunky sauce. You can bottle it and keep it in the fridge for two weeks, but we usually use it up immediately.

Flatten the chickens by cutting through the back bone and bashing them flat. Score the flesh on the breasts and thighs (I know this is not how it should be done, but it helps the marinade penetrate to the bone).

Place in a dish, coat liberally in the sauce, and marinate over night. Remove from the fridge about an hour before cooking.

Light your fire and burn it down to moderate coals. This is a long, slow cook, so it's best on a braai with a lid, like a kettle. The sugar in the marinade will make the skin burn easily, so keep checking. It will take about 35–45 minutes depending on the size of the birds. Every time you check on them, baste marinade from the marinating dish.

Serve with fresh lemon and chips.

Makes 500 ml sauce

SHISANYAMA

South Africans seem to think that we invented cooking over fires. We invented the braai after all. However, our very evolution as humans rests with applying fire to food. I once read somewhere that one of the things that sets us apart from other species is the ability to cook.

A braai is not the only way of cooking over fire, but for us there is nothing like standing round a fire grilling meat. There are many approaches to a braai, and one of my favourites is the shisanyama.

The term means 'burn meat', and if you go into any working-class area or township in this country, you will find some kind of shisanyama.

There's always a precinct in a community, even in informal settlements, where a couple of roadside grills are set up by locals as part of a thriving alternative economy. They provide some individuals an income, and for the community it's a gathering place. You can feel the heartbeat of the place at the fire, and pick up on local gossip and characters.

Some shisanyamas like Mzoli's in Cape Town's Gugulethu have developed into iconic establishments. It's a bit of a tourist trap though, so I prefer the roadside ones that spring up in local communities like Khayamandi in Stellenbosch.

Any kind of meat is cooked on a shisanyama: wors, beef, freshly killed chicken and especially brisket. A roadside shisanyama taught me that you can actually braai a brisket. In South Africa the brisket cut is something we slow cook and braise for hours. Americans take the same cut for slow-smoking until it becomes tender. In Khayamandi, I ate brisket thinly sliced and spiced with the bone in and fat out, cooked over open coals. It's much cheaper than fillet and offers delicious, big and bold, beefy flavours. No wonder people love it so much.

SPICE RUB FOR BRAAIED BRISKET

750 g brisket

SPICE RUB
50 g sugar
150 g coarse salt
4 sprigs thyme
2 cloves garlic
1 tbsp coriander seeds
2 juniper berries
1 tbsp paprika
2 tsp cayenne pepper
2 bay leaf
2 tsp black peppercorns

Slice the brisket as thinly as possible.

Put all the rub ingredients in a mortar and pestle or spice grinder and grind to a rough powder. Coat the meat generously, rub and leave it to 'cure' for at least an hour and a half before cooking over moderate coals. Make sure that you crisp up any fatty bits.

Don't be fancy – eat it with your fingers!

You can keep any left-over rub in an airtight container for up to 10 days.

MEALIES

Just as maize is the staple food of southern Africa, grilled mealies are its fast food. I absolutely love those roadside vendors who roast and hawk mealies to travellers. They seem to be disappearing now, because I see them less and less on road trips around the country. That customary aunty roasting mealies is not so much a fixture at bus stops any more.

I wonder if the growth of chain takeaways around taxi ranks and other hotspots working people congregate has put an end to that. Perhaps in a modernising society, they aren't seen as hygienic or healthy, but I think those hawkers offer a perfect meal on the go. A grilled white mealie is a meal in itself. It's deliciously nutty, very filling, and you can eat it with one hand.

Whenever I travelled through the old Transkei, I'd look out for one of these aunties to get a mealie or two. If you asked for salt they'd charge an extra rand. For Aromat it was R1.50. Who eats mealies without a good shake of Aromat?

Where I still see them on is in small towns and less modernised centres. Like a shisanyama there's usually a fire in a simple half-drum with a big blackened pot on one side and a grid on the other. Mealies are first boiled in the pot to cook them through, then are finished over the coals to give them their earthy chargrilled flavour.

It's such a pity that this tradition is disappearing. Eating mealies has become part of our braai tradition, where we boil cobs of sweetcorn and finish them on the braai with some kind of buttery, spicy basting. They are easy to eat and manage because of the smaller and softer kernels.

They are increasingly a feature at the township shisanyamas, and I love ordering a couple to have with my brisket. At home around a braai, I've developed a recipe for a dukkah to spice the sweetcorn up and keep the tradition close to my heart.

MEALIES WITH DUKKAH MAYO

DUKKAH SPICE

50 g almonds

50 g macadamia nuts

½ tsp dried chilli flakes

1 tsp coriander seeds

2 tsp black sesame seeds

2 tsp white sesame seeds

1 tsp peppercorns

1 tsp caraway seeds

1 tsp cumin seeds

1 tsp fennel seeds

1 tsp coarse salt

MAYONNAISE

1 egg yolk

2 tsp Dijon mustard

1 tsp vinegar

250 ml vegetable oil

salt

few drops of fresh
 lemon juice

15 ml water

4 mealies, husked
 and cleaned

vegetable oil

In a dry pan over moderate heat, toast the nuts and spices together until fragrant and aromatic, about 3–4 minutes, stirring continuously. Now transfer everything to a mortar and pestle or spice grinder and crush to a rough powder.

For the mayo, whisk the yolk, mustard and vinegar together. Add the oil a little at a time while whisking vigorously. As soon as an emulsion starts to form, you can add the oil a little faster. Whisk until the mayo is firm. Season with a pinch of salt and lemon juice. Add the water a little at a time to make the mayo creamy. Make this in advance. (It makes more than you will need and will keep for a week in the fridge.)

Cook the mealies in a large pot of salted boiling water for 15 minutes. Drain, dry and cook over medium coals, turning regularly until the mealies start to brown all over. You can cook them in the kitchen if you heat a pan with a dash of oil over a moderate heat and grill the mealies until brown.

Combine 2/3 of the dukkah mixture with the mayonnaise. Serve this spooned over the mealies. Offer the balance of the dry spice separately for extra seasoning.

Serves 4

BOEREWORS ROLL

Boerewors was known as Mom's night off from cooking in the Basson home. We would either throw it on the braai or steam it dry in a pan with water, which meant no fat or oil. It was then served with pap and a lekker spicy sheba (tomato, chilli and onion relish) and for breakfast we would simply fry the eggs in the left over pan jus, giving the eggs a lovely meaty flavour.

Boerewors is an essential part of every South African braai and doesn't go without emotion. No one can resist the smell of a Boerie outside the supermarket on a Saturday morning; it is an absolute South African treat. Boeries are one of those things that seem to feed the masses, like the story of the fish and bread, boerie rolls are sold and served by their hundreds at rugby matches, camps and on Saturday morning shopping expeditions.

The boerewors is a fresh sausage born out of necessity, originating from the Dutch based on an older traditional Dutch sausage called the verse worst. The Germans also made them for survival purposes during harsh times. For a South African twist on the sausage, we add a lot more salt and let it cure and dry to produce our famous droë wors (dry wors), which is popular in its own right as a snack.

Boerewors comes in different lengths and sizes and is very region specific. Here in the Western Cape we produce the Grabouw boerewors which has its own spice variety and recipe. Although boerewors must contain at least 90 per cent meat – always containing beef, as well as lamb or pork or a mixture of lamb and pork. The other 10% is made up of spices and other ingredients.

The best boerewors roll you'll ever taste is in the Builders Warehouse car park outside Cape Town. Like so many other traditional Afrikaner foods, the boerewors in a roll has been turned by many into an economic survival mechanism. There are many ooms and tannies putting the kids through school or paying the rent by selling boerie rolls at pop-up stalls around the country.

On the first season of the Ultimate Braai Master we had a boerewors cook-off at the Shark Tank in Durban as one of the contestants' challenges. One of the teams prepared this incredible bacon, banana and garlic mayo boerie roll. What a combo. I have used it a few times and it really deserves to be preserved for posterity.

BANANA REPUBLIC BOERIE

WORS ROLL
4 x 150 g lengths of boerewors
4 hot dog rolls
2 bananas
8 rashers bacon

CRISPY ONIONS
2 medium onions, thickly sliced
100 ml milk
100 g flour
pinch of salt
paprika

MUSTARD AND GARLIC MAYO
1 egg yolk
1 tsp Dijon mustard
1 tbsp wholegrain mustard
1 tsp vinegar
2 cloves garlic, crushed
250 ml vegetable oil
salt
a few drops of fresh lemon juice
15 ml water

Grill the boerewors over medium to low coals or on a gas grill. As the fat drips, there will be some flare-ups and smoke that add to the flavour. Depending on the thickness, cook the wors for 3 minutes per side. Keep it juicy.

Grill the bacon and banana on the same fire – it should only take a minute.

Toss the onions through the milk and drain. Mix the flour, salt and paprika and toss the onions in this seasoned flour. Fry them in a deep fryer at 160°C until golden brown and crisp. Drain on kitchen towel until you need them.

For the mayo, whisk the yolk, both mustards and vinegar together. Add the oil a little at a time while whisking vigorously. As soon as an emulsion starts to form, you can add the oil a little faster. Whisk until the mayo it is firm. Season with a pinch of salt and lemon juice. Add the water a little at a time to make the mayo creamy. Make in advance, it will keep for a week in the fridge.

To finish, slice the rolls open, smear generously with the mayo, pop in the wors and top with the grilled bacon and banana, and finally with the crisp onions. Feast.

Serves 4

PIES

The first and foremost go-to food of drunken South Africans is the pie. I know because I have been drunk before.

You can get them anywhere. The corner tea room or 24-hour service station always has a pie-warmer with a couple of dodgy pies with gloopy fillings. No student party, it seems, is quite complete without the tableau of a couple of mates standing around, swaying noticeably, and scoffing a pie. The crackly sound of the packet is the swansong of a great night out for many people. Thing is, you never know what's in 'em. They've become synonymous with bad food and unpleasant fillings.

When I was growing up, there was nothing as delicious as my Ma's chicken pie. Made traditionally, with a whole chicken (she achieves the perfect balance between white and dark meat), mushrooms and sago to add to the consistency and to bind the pie together. It was finished off with my favourite part of the dish – the puff pastry. I used to love the corners which always had the thicker bit of the pastry.

Her pies were the kind that came in a big dish. You'd cut slices out like a cake and eat it with veg or salad with a knife and fork. The pie of choice for dronkgatte are those single-serving, eat-in-the-carpark-while-the-world-spins kind of pies.

My Ma and a few small artisanal bakeries still uphold the honour and pleasure of the pie though. Done right, they are the most convenient and potentially delicious convenience food. What better road-trip food is there?

When Mareli and I travel through Elgin, in the Overberg, we find it difficult to choose between the Peregrine or Houwhoek farmstall. Their pies are top quality and incredibly delicious. Similarly, we can never drive past Oude Meul in Riviersonderend without stopping for a pie.

I still like to eat a pie that I can hold with one hand, and a lot of delicious leftovers go into Cornish pastie-style pies at my house. In the restaurant, though, we walk a line between the two styles by offering a dish pie with a pastry topping that comes in a single-serving portion.

VENISON PIE

It is best to make the pie filling at least a day ahead. That's why leftovers are always so good for pies. The pastry is best made a day ahead too. This recipe makes enough for a lot of pies, but everything here freezes fabulously, so you are building the pies of the future.

FILLING
2.5 kg springbok shin
   on the bone
2 carrots
2 onions
1 tbsp salt
1 whole chilli
750 ml wine
500 ml fresh tomato puree
3 cloves garlic
2 bay leaves
peel of half a lemon
sprig fresh thyme

PASTRY
500 g flour
125 g butter
salt
250 ml cold water
half a lemon, juiced
500 g butter

Have the springbok cut into stewing portions. Peel and quarter the onions, scrub and chunk the carrots. Put everything for the filling in a heavy pot like a Le Creuset with a lid in an oven at 100°C and leave it there for 6 hours. Check occasionally that there's still enough liquid. If it looks a bit dry towards the end, add a bit of boiling water.

When it comes out of the oven, use a carving fork to carefully remove all the bones. If it's still a bit too juicy, place the pot on the stovetop and reduce the juice to concentrate the flavor into a thick ragu.

For the puff pastry, blitz the flour, butter and a pinch of salt to form fine crumbs. Stir the lemon juice into the water and pour it steadily into the crumbs while the processor is running. When it is just coming together, turn it out onto a floured surface. Knead until smooth, form a ball and wrap it in cling wrap. Pop it in the fridge for at least 2 hours.

Roll out the dough on a floured surface until it's about 20 x 60 cm. Cut your cold 500 g block of butter into 5 mm slices down the length. Lay these in a single layer over two thirds of the pastry. Fold the remaining one third flap back over the middle third of the pastry. Now fold the sandwiched bit over the remaining layer of buttered pastry. It's like folding an A4 letter in three to fit in an official rectangular envelope.

Fold this parcel in half and roll out to the original size again. Do the letter fold of a third and a third, fold in half and roll out again. Fold again, wrap in cling wrap and place in the fridge for 2 hours. Do the folding and rolling process again three times and put it back in the fridge before you use it for the pies.

To assemble a fancy pie, fill a little ovenproof dish or small skillet with about 200 g of ragu. Cover with a disk of puff pastry. Brush with egg wash and bake in a preheated oven at 180°C until the pastry is crisp and golden (about 20 minutes).

Makes 12 or so

PANNEKOEK

A lot of my childhood food memories were made around treats. I've mentioned that I was a scrappy eater and I used to drive my Ma crazy. There was always room for something sweet though.

Growing up in a tightly knit community in Nelspruit, I was always going to some or other fund-raising event. Standard offerings (one of my favourite) at church bazaars or school fetes was pannekoek.

I love the sight and bustle of kerk bazaar tannies on a Saturday morning cooking up pancakes by the thousand. A queue is a definite guarantee of quality, but it also talks to our love of those sugar-and-cinnamon-dusted indulgences. The trick, if you come across one, is to order 5 or 6; you'll regret it if you don't.

That in itself is quite fun. There's a money Tannie, a cooking Tannie, and the Tannie who sugars, rolls and serves your treat. It's all such a firm tradition with rules and methods worked out across thousands and thousands of communal events across South Africa. Pannekoek or Dutch pancake is a style of pancake that I guess came with settlers from the Netherlands. It's sort of like a French crêpe, and the pannekoek brought here by Dutch settlers probably shares its origins from the north west of France.

The world famous French crêpe is called crêpe Suzette. It's origin, like those tannies at the bazaar, still inspires me. Apparently crêpe Suzette was created by mistake by a fourteen-year-old assistant waiter preparing a dessert in a chafing dish for the Prince of Wales in Paris in 1895. One of his dinner guests was a beautiful French girl named Suzette. The young waiter – perhaps totally overawed by the company – accidentally set fire to some cordials he had added to the dish. Thinking it was ruined, he tasted it and was so pleased with the result that he served it to the delighted diners.

The waiter tried to name it after the prince, but the chivalrous oke refused and named it crêpe Suzette for the pretty girl at his side instead. Thus was born and baptised this confection, one taste of which, he really believed, would reform a cannibal into a civilised gentleman.

I've been playing with this recipe for a long time. It kind of gentrifies a church bazaar pannekoek by introducing it to some alcohol and a chaffing dish. We keep it local by adding naartjies and Van der Hum too.

CRÊPE SUZIE!

PANCAKES
375 ml flour
pinch of salt
½ tsp baking powder
250 ml milk
125 ml buttermilk
125 ml water
2 eggs
30 ml vegetable oil

CRÊPE SUZIE SAUCE
3 tbsp sugar
2 tbsp butter
2 oranges, zested and juiced
2 oranges, segmented
2 naartjies, segmented
2 lemons, zested and juiced
45 ml good brandy
100 ml Van der Hum liqueur
4 crushed cardamom pods

Sift all the dry ingredients together into one bowl, and whisk the milk, buttermilk, water, eggs and oil together in another. Slowly pour the wet ingredients into the dry ingredients, whisking continuously to form a smooth batter. Rest the batter for at least 60 minutes (but preferably overnight) in the fridge.

Rub a good quality 24 cm non-stick pan with a drop of vegetable oil. Heat to a moderate heat and add approximately 80 ml of the pancake batter. Roll the pan around to spread the batter equally. Cook until lightly brown on the one side. Flip over and lightly brown the other side. Fold the pancakes into quarters allocating 2 pancakes per person.

Gently heat a large skillet, big enough to fit 8 folded pancakes. Place the sugar in the dry skillet and let it caramelise lightly. Add the butter and stir until the butter has dissolved. Add the orange and lemon juice. Stir vigorously to form a citrus syrup.

Carefully place the folded pancakes in the pan and coat them in the syrup. Add the orange and lemon zest. Tilt the pan into the flame and add the brandy and Van der Hum, so that the pancakes flambé. When the flame dies off, add the orange segments.

Serve immediately with good-quality vanilla ice cream.

Serves 4

SOUT TERT

A sout tert is a beautiful boere-tannie thing. It's kind of a quiche, but it is so far removed from that refined, French dish, that I shudder to make the comparison. In this instance the word sout in the name does not refer to salt. It's not a salty tart. Rather, the term sout is used to indicate savoury. So sout tert is basically a savoury tart.

Savoury tarts are a staple of the little community institution known as a tuisnywerheid. These little home industry shops allow housewives or stay-at-home mums to earn a little income from their cooking or baking skills.

My Ma baked for the main home industry store in Nelspruit, and did pretty well for herself. She was more of a cake baker, so I never came home to rows of sout terte on the kitchen counters, but there were plenty of delivery runs and stock appraisal opportunities.

Where the tannie fantasticness comes into things is what the aunties put in their sout tert. In typical penny-pinching style, the ingredients are often mean rather than generous. Just as tinned asparagus is used to destroy the '50s version of quiche in countless South African homes, so have tinned viennas oppressed the sout tert for generations.

I love this contradiction. All the ladies vie with each other to be proclaimed the best baker in the district. It means so much, they gossip about it after bible study, or at the church bazaar. But suggest that they try some cubed gammon in their sout tert, or some good farm eggs, and their lips go all thin with disapproval.

While I was in London, I worked for a good part of my stay there at the legendary Chez Bruce. It was an incredible experience that taught me so much about running and working in a contemporary kitchen.

One of the popular dishes on the menu – something I must have made a thousand times – was a fabulous, quiche-like onion tart. It reminded me so much of home and sout tert. I think a little homesick part of me might have yearned for the taste of tinned viennas in that onion tart. The next recipe is my version of Chez Bruce's onion tart with a nostalgic nod to sout tert.

CHEZ BRUCE ONION TART

SHORTCRUST PASTRY
1 cup cake flour
125 g butter
1 egg, beaten
pinch of salt
pinch of paprika

FILLING
1.5 kg onions, sliced
250 g butter
12 egg yolks
500 ml cream
1 tsp salt
1 tsp thyme, picked

Rub the flour, salt, paprika and butter together. Now add the egg, mix through and gently push together into a dough. Cover in a bowl and refrigerate overnight.

Preheat your oven to 180°C.

On a lightly floured surface, roll out the pastry to about 3 mm thick. Line your fluted quiche pan with the pastry, leaving at least 2 cm pastry overlapping the edges. Trim off the excess pastry.

Line the pastry with baking paper and fill with dry beans and blind-bake for 20 minutes. Remove the paper and baking beans and return to the oven for 5 minutes, to ensure the pastry is cooked through. Remove and cool completely.

For the filling, sweat off the onions, butter and salt in a large pot over a low heat. They should sweat very slowly over a 2-hour period. Stir occasionally. The onions should be very soft and have a light caramel colour. Drain them thoroughly in a sieve, and leave to cool completely.

Fill the pastry shell with the onions. Beat together the egg yolks, cream and salt and pour the mixture over the onions. Sprinkle the thyme over the tart.

Bake at 130°C for 50 minutes, until the tart is lightly set. Remove from the oven and trim off the excess pastry.

Cool completely and serve with crisp salad leaves.

Serves 6 to 8

GUAVAS

KOO brand tinned guavas are as iconic to our food culture as Lucky Star tinned pilchards. There was always a tin or two in the pantry when I was a kid. Everyone else's mom also had KOO guavas in their grocery cupboard.

The thing about them is that they are sweet and taste lekker. You were never stuck for dessert when there were KOO guavas in the house. Guavas and custard was the classic '70s dessert of middle-class South Africa. It was easy and quick, and completely ignored the glory of fresh guavas in season.

Right near our Spice Route venue, there's an intersection on the road from Klapmuts to Stellenbosch where fruit and veg hawkers ply their trade. I love buying from these guys, because the produce is always seasonal and fresh. When it's guava season we buy bags and bags of them to poach and use in all sorts of ways.

My best is guavas and custard. We make a more cheffy version though, by poaching fresh guavas and making an amazing baked custard.

POACHED GUAVAS WITH MUSCADEL CUSTARD

GUAVAS
6 firm, ripe guavas
400 ml water
1 cup sugar
1 stick cinnamon

CUSTARD
2 eggs
4 egg yolks
¼ cup sugar
250 ml cream
125 ml Muscadel

100 g roasted cashew nuts
30 ml pickled ginger

1 tsp thyme, picked
pinch of salt

Peel and halve the guavas and scoop out the seeds. Place the water, sugar and cinnamon in a saucepan and bring to a boil over medium heat, stirring occasionally. Reduce the heat and simmer for 15 minutes. Add the guava halves and return to the boil. Partially cover the pot and reduce the heat to a gentle simmer until the guavas are tender but not too soft. Remove from the heat and cool. They will keep in the fridge for a week in the syrup.

For the custard, cream the eggs, yolks and sugar until light and fluffy. Bring the cream just to the boil, stir in the Muscadel and immediately pour steadily into the egg mixture, whisking constantly until combined.

Divide the mixture equally into 4 jars and bake in a bain marie at 160°C, until the custard is lightly set (15–20 minutes).

Chill the custard. Serve with the guavas, a little poaching juice, roasted cashew nuts and ginger finely sliced in long strips.

Serves 4 to 6

KOEKSISTER

South Africans are such traditionalists. There's a monument to the koeksister in the Afrikaner enclave of Orania which recalls a folk tradition of baking them to raise funds for the building of churches and schools. Even today, school bake sales and church fêtes are not complete without at least one koeksister stand run by a staunch tannie. Every town or community has its very own champion koeksister tannie – ever in competition to stay the best.

The koeksister itself touches and changes many lives, even at a city robot. There's a man I buy from regularly in Cape Town. After losing his job, he started selling his sister's homemade koeksisters at an intersection in the city. Twenty years later, he has a huge network of loyal customers who help pay the bills and keep him going. In fact, I know a couple of chefs who use his koeksisters for desserts and personal stash. These babies are so good and affordable that it makes no sense to make them yourself.

I can't even begin to imagine how many households have been fed by the proceeds from koeksister sales. I reckon that in every office block in South Africa there's either someone visiting with a basket of them for sale, or someone in the office is making them for extra cash on the side. Koeksisters are the root of this sort of alternative economy among working middle class Afrikaners. Something extra for the holidays, or school fees, or the electricity bill.

Traditionally, we enjoy these yummy and messy delights after lunch with a freshly brewed coffee. Many people who aren't steeped in the tradition get koeksisters all wrong. They end up in the fridge as midnight cheats, and in a new eating culture that's wary of both sugar and gluten, they're a no-no.

Let's face it, koeksisters are prepared by deep-frying plaited sausages of dough in oil, then soaking them in cold sugar syrup. This makes them a very occasional treat for the health-conscious. My recipe for koeksister ice cream is meant for special occasions, but people love it. I don't bother making the koeksisters myself, as I'd rather support the local koeksister economy. Get to know your koeksister vendor; there's probably quite a story there.

KOEKSISTER ICE CREAM

400 ml milk
600 ml cream
¾ cup sugar
ground cinnamon
10 egg yolks
200 g koeksisters,
   chopped up

Bring the milk, cream, half of the sugar and a pinch of cinnamon to the boil. (The sugar is heavier than the milk and cream mixture, and will 'fall' to the bottom of the pan and prevent the milk and cream from burning.)

While the milk mixture is coming to temperature, cream the egg yolks and the rest of the sugar in a mixer (we like Kitchen Aid) at high speed. Adjust the speed of the mixer to a lower setting and add the scalding milk mixture to the eggs to combine into a smooth custard. There will be enough heat in the milk mixture to cook the egg yolks in the custard.

Cool the mixture completely, then churn in an ice cream machine until smooth.

When you are reaching the end of your churn, add the pieces of koeksister to mix through. Spoon into a container with a lid and freeze until required.

There is of course a cheat version of this recipe. You just buy your favourite vanilla ice cream. Soften it enough to mix in the chopped koeksister and then re-freeze. We also do this with left-over Christmas pudding.

Serves 6 to 8

INGREDIENTS
(bestandele en spens)

INGREDIENTS

In the section about Gatsbys from **page 87**, I mentioned the Epping market where we shop for a lot of the basic fresh produce ingredients we use in the restaurants. There's so much going on with farming and bringing incredible produce to market in South Africa, but that's only the beginning of the journey.

There are literally dozens of producers who are specialising now in obscure or very particular varieties of fresh produce. There's an Italian guy we work with who set himself up to grow broad beans. All kinds of kitchen gardeners are starting to bring obscure things to market as local restauranteurs seek more and more interesting stuff to feed our mushrooming food culture.

By now you can probably tell that I'm a steak, potatoes and cauliflower guy at heart, but new ingredients fascinate me. I love working with new stuff using old methods or classic flavour combinations. As people bring in new things and the restaurants use them, home cooks go looking for it in the shops. So restaurants drive the initial demands and slowly these odd things become commonplace. The thing is, with our amazing soil, diverse climates and incredible ingenuity, we can grow any product or raise any livestock in South Africa.

Take for instance the beetroot we use in the salad on **page 148**. We used to get a whole range of baby heirloom beetroot from a speciality grower in Porterville, Western Cape. His name was Steve Botha and he called himself the Magic Man. He was so proud of his crop and people were blown away by the diversity and flavour of his produce when we presented it in dishes at Overture. It proved so popular that now you can find candy-stripe and golden beetroot at dozens of outlets.

Tomatoes are the same. When I was a kid, you got round red tomatoes. Now there are people growing heritage varieties in all kinds of shapes and colours. Check out your local Woolies and count how many different kinds of tomatoes you can find on any given day. It's amazing.

I have to say, though, I still love those early mornings at Epping market with the farmers surrounded by potatoes and cauliflowers, and big, round, red tomatoes.

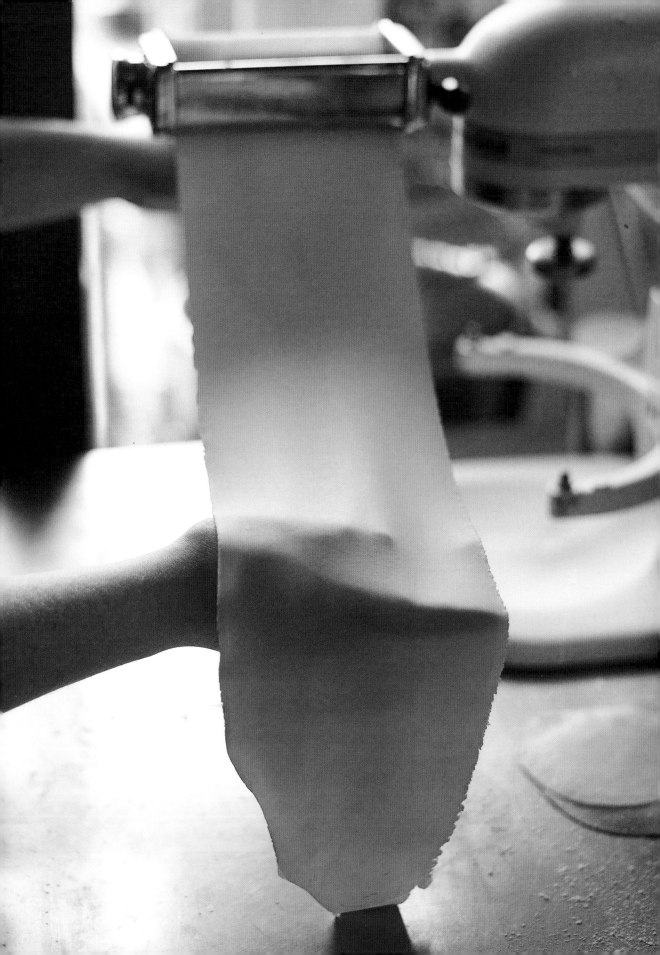

TOMATO PARMESAN RAVIOLI

Tomatoes were always just tomatoes, until I ate them in a ravioli at Tristan restaurant in Majorca. I came back and reproduced it for the Overture menu. It was that good. Tomatoes are so versatile, delivering sweetness and acidity in one package.

In this dish, the beautiful symbiosis of combining tomatoes with basil is showcased perfectly.

PASTA
2 cups 'OO' flour
4 eggs, beaten

TOMATO FILLING
2 onions, finely chopped
2 garlic cloves, minced
75 ml olive oil
1.5 kg tomatoes, quartered
handful fresh basil
50 g grated Parmesan
salt
knob of butter

Put the flour in a food processor and, while it is running, pour in the eggs. Switch off when the dough resembles coarse crumbs, and turn it out onto a clean surface to knead until smooth. Wrap it in plastic and rest in the fridge for at least an hour before use.

Starting at No.1 and working through each setting on the machine, roll out the pasta dough, folding several times. With a 12 cm scone cutter, make pasta disks. Pile them as you go, with a little flour to prevent sticking.

In a heavy saucepan, sweat off the onions and garlic in olive oil until lightly caramelised.

Meanwhile, whiz the tomatoes in a blender until smooth. Pass the pulp through a sieve to remove skin or seeds, and add it to the onions with the torn basil leaves. Bring to a boil then simmer until it forms a firm, thick paste. Remove from the saucepan to cool completely, then stir in the grated Parmesan.

On a lightly floured or semolina-dusted surface, lay half the disks flat. Brush each with a little water, being careful not to wet them too much. Spoon a little tomato mixture onto the centre of each disk and cover with a second disk. Press the edges down to seal the ravioli.

Note* Try to push all the air bubbles out of the pasta pocket, and work quickly to prevent it drying out. Lay them out on a semolina-dusted surface as you work.

Bring a large pot of salted water to the boil. Add the ravioli, a few at a time, to cook for about 90 seconds each. Don't crowd the water. Remove with a slotted spoon, toss with butter and serve immediately with shavings of Parmesan.

We serve the ravioli with a fresh tomato and basil vinaigrette and black olive pesto.

Serves 8 to 12

BEETROOT AMASI CREAM CHEESE SALAD

Like most South Africans I grew up eating pickled beetroot from a jar. It never rocked my world. The real revelation for me as a young chef came when I ate beetroot with sour cream for the first time – I think it was in London. I loved how this sweet, earthy root was offset against the acidity from the sour cream.

A thought about the unique flavour of amasi (fermented milk – a poor man's food) and beetroot led to the creation of one of the early hit dishes at Overture. We served dried amasi with different styles of beetroot.

1 L amasi
salt
squeeze of lemon juice
12 assorted baby
  heirloom beetroots

Line a conical strainer with a clean muslin cloth or a thin tea towel. Pour in the amasi and refrigerate overnight. The liquid will drain off slowly leaving the delicious, creamy, acidic whey or milk solids behind. It's very much like making labneh or ricotta.

Remove the cloth from the strainer, place the milk solids in a bowl, season with salt and lemon juice. The amasi cream cheese also flavours really well with a pinch of roasted, crushed cumin seeds.

Simmer the beetroot in salted water. Once soft, remove from the heat and allow the beetroot to cool in their cooking water. Peel the beetroots, the cooking should have loosened their skins. Depending on the varietal, quarter or thinly slice them. We would quarter the solid coloured ones and thinly slice the variegated or candy-striped ones to vary appearance and texture in the salad.

Dress with a spoonful of mustard dressing (see page 192) or a vinaigrette. Serve with dollops of amasi cream cheese among or around your artistically arranged beetroot.

At Overture we added complexity with beetroot puree, beetroot powder and dried beetroot shavings. None of this is essential, the crux of the dish is earthy beetroot with amasi.

Serves 4

VENISON

My dad used to make his own biltong. He would go out and shoot an impala, then butcher it in the garage and make all this amazing biltong for us to eat. It required using vinegar, spices and salt.

Salt. The simple fact that salt preserves food has enabled humanity to discover the world. Salted cod changed the face of our planet. When I think about that I realise how much food knowledge was around me growing up. I just didn't truly grasp it.

In South Africa, biltong was first produced to fill the pantry for harder times, or as trail food for the great trek. During the Boer wars it travelled in saddlebags to be re-constituted in stews. Now it is the ubiquitous South African snack food item. We love biltong.

So my dad would make biltong in the garage, with the carcasses hanging right there. Choice cuts would end up in the oven or on the braai, a memory that led to me sourcing impala loin for our tartare dish at Overture.

The impala is specifically a Lowveld gazelle as opposed to the springbok, which is wider ranging. I wanted that for our menu, to acknowledge my own food heritage and a memory I hold dear.

We explore the heritage of biltong by soft-curing various cuts of beef and venison. It reminds me so much of my dad and the hours he would spend in the garage in Nelspruit. I always roll my eyes at middle-class South Africans who have a lot to say about how black people slaughter goats in the back yard, yet many Afrikaners think it's perfectly acceptable cutting up a bok in their garage.

IMPALA TARTARE

300 g impala loin,
  hand-minced
6 baby gherkins, chopped
2 tbsp capers, chopped
1 small red onion,
  finely chopped
Tabasco, to taste
Worcestershire sauce, to taste
80 ml homemade mayonnaise
  (page 102)
2 tsp chives, finely chopped
juice of half a lemon
salt and pepper

For the tartare place the meat, gherkins, capers and onion in a mixing bowl.

Add the Tabasco, the Worcestershire sauce and mayonnaise then mix everything through thoroughly. Add the chives and lemon juice. Season with salt and pepper, and make sure everything is combined.

Serve as a starter with fresh radishes and ciabatta (page 82).

Serves 4

SOFT-CURED BILTONG

1.5 kg sirloin
½ cup coarse salt
45 ml vinegar
3 tbsp brown sugar
30 ml Worcestershire sauce
1 pinch chilli flakes
1 tbsp coriander seeds,
   crushed
1 tsp cumin seeds
1 tsp black peppercorns,
   crushed

Trim the sirloin and split in half, lengthways, keeping as much fat on as possible.

Mix the rest of the ingredients in a bowl and add the sirloin. Get in there and rub the coarser bits of the marinade into the meat. When you are happy that the sirloin is truly coated and soaked, cover the bowl with a plate or lid and pop it in the fridge.

For the next day or so, check on the bowl regularly, turning the sirloin over in the marinade when you do. After at least 24 hours in the fridge, thread a piece of string through the fatty part of each piece of meat. In winter you can hang the sirloin in a cool, drafty area; however, in summer you should hang it in your fridge or in a biltong dryer.

As long as you don't dry it too much and the centre stays moist, you can keep it hanging. The length of time is dependent on the humidity of your surroundings.

Once you are happy with how dry the meat is, pop it into the freezer to firm up before slicing.

My favourite way to eat it is with Parmesan shavings and garden greens. We served it in the restaurant with pickled celeriac, shaved romanesco, garden greens, anchovies and black olives.

Makes over 1 kg soft biltong

PORK

Some people think I'm a bit strange, because there appears to be a contradiction going on with me. Mareli and I share our home with three dogs and a pig called Spek. He came to me as a very small piglet and we have a very special relationship. I'm often asked how I can eat pork when I have a pet pig. It's simple: Spekkie is for loving, not eating. He's my mate.

However, having Spek in my life has made me extremely sensitive about the way farmed pigs are raised and the conditions in which they are kept.

I am a fan of the pig. I think they are amazing animals. They are intelligent, useful farm animals and I reckon the world is a happier place since they were domesticated. I remember reading in John Seymour's classic book on self-sufficiency about using pigs to clear scrub. He wrote that all you needed to clear dense scrub and ready it for planting or other use is a couple of pigs. Fence the area off, throw in a few handfuls of maize, put the pigs in and they will reduce the area to bare ground very quickly looking for the maize. Living with a healthy, hungry pig, I believe it.

So pigs are useful to farmers for many things, but they are also delicious to eat. We work with Sweetwell piggery on the R44 outside Stellenbosch to supply Overture Restaurant. It helps that they are just down the road from the restaurant, but Sweetwell is a recognised stud piggery. They are committed to best farming practices, not adding hormones to feed, ensuring the physical and mental needs of their livestock as a primary concern and so on.

It's a small operation, and the Cronje family are incredibly obliging to our occasionally bizarre requests. They will provide unusual cuts, brine certain things and always ensure that we have amazing pork products for our diners.

If you ask me what the best cut of pork is, I'd say the belly without hesitation. All the piggy flavour, meatiness and fat is bound up there in a perfect package. For me eating a pork belly that is prepared well is a sensual journey.

BEER BRAISED PORK BELLY

1 pork belly, whole

BRINE
½ cup sugar
½ cup salt
2.5 L water
2 thyme sprigs
2 cloves of garlic
1 tsp coriander seeds
1 tsp cumin seeds
½ tsp cloves
1 star anise pod
2 dried chillies

BRAISING LIQUID
1 onion, sliced
2 carrots, chopped
2 garlic cloves
2 thyme sprigs
3 L beer
1 L water

GINGER HONEY GLAZE
100 g honey
50 g butter
20 g chopped ginger

24 baby heirloom carrots

Remove the fat from the pork belly. Make the brine by dissolving the salt and sugar in the water and add the herbs and spices. Submerge the belly in the brine for 48 hours. You will need a weight to keep it below the surface of the liquid, and it should be refrigerated the whole time.

To braise, remove the belly from the brine and rub off any excess spices. Roll and tie with butcher's string to hold the shape. Place in a large pot with the vegetables, aromatics, beer and water. Cover the pot with foil and cover with a lid so no moisture can escape. Cook in an oven at 85°C for 12 hours. Remove from the oven and cool in the braising liquid.

Remove the string and roll the belly in cling wrap to form a nice log shape. Refrigerate for at least 4 hours until the belly is firmly set.

For the glaze, cook all the ingredients in a saucepan over a moderate heat until the butter is emulsified, and it starts to look syrupy. Remove from the heat.

Preheat your oven to 160°C.

Clean and blanch the carrots until tender, then toss them in the warm glaze to coat. Transfer the carrots to an ovenproof dish and reserve the glaze. Roast in the oven for 30 minutes, being careful not to burn the honey.

Slice a disk of pork belly, 2–3 cm thick and crisp it in a non-stick pan over a high heat. Serve with 4 carrots per portion and a drizzle of the reserved glaze. Vark en soet wortels. We also like serving the belly with dollop of salsa verde and carrot puree.

Serves 6

WHOLE ROAST LAMB LIVER WITH SORREL

I grew up eating shoulder, leg or chops of lamb. That's what I thought lamb was about. It was only when I started cooking for a living that I realised that the best bits of most animals are the ones other people are uncomfortable preparing or eating. Cooking delicious things with offal became a challenge.

If you really want to challenge yourself to be a gourmand, you need to look at the whole animal, not just a pack of chops from the supermarket.

400 g fresh lambs liver
vegetable oil
100 g butter
sprig of thyme
2 cloves garlic, bruised

Pre-heat the oven to 180°C.

Make sure that the liver is clean and that the membrane on the outside is removed.

Heat a heavy-bottomed pan with a drop of oil. Seal the liver on both sides. Add the butter to the pan and add the thyme and garlic. Baste the liver on the stove continuously for 2 minutes.

Turn over and pop into the oven, continue to baste in the oven every minute or so. Remove from the oven after about 10 minutes and allow to rest in the pan with the butter.

To serve, carve a couple of slices per person and dress with some pan juices and butter from roasting. We love serving this with parsnip puree, roast parsnips and green beans, but fresh sorrel or red-vein sorrel work well too.

MUSSELS WITH BEER, BACON & SEAWEED

Mareli and I talk a lot about the future. We think about what we are working on, what we've done, what we'd like to do. Sometimes when we've been under pressure on a big function or event we dream about giving it all up and opting for a quieter life.

The idea that comes up again and again is opening a mussel bar. If we ever hit a wall and lose everything, or just decide to throw the towel in, that will be our plan. There's such a lure for me in the idea of a simple little eatery where we serve one ingredient brilliantly, and my ingredient of choice would be mussels.

There's a bit of history here, because when we were on family holidays at the beach, my dad taught me to catch little fish in rock pools using mussel shells and meat from limpets. At the time, though, I would never so much as try a mussel, let alone sit down to a meal of them. What a wasted opportunity.

Luckily my later curiosity about food finally did introduce me to mussels. Luckily. I just love the flavour profile. The flavour versus cost value they deliver means these humble little molluscs punch way above their weight. They are also available straight from the beach if you know where and when to go musselling.

I'd rather eat or serve mussels than abalone any day. And maybe one day I might. Perhaps something based on a Belgian moule frites restaurant. Mussels sautéed in wine or crumbed on the half shell with chunky hand-cut chips. But that's a dream for another time.

100 g butter
250 g belly bacon, cubed
1 large onion, diced
3 cloves of garlic, thinly sliced
400 ml beer
3 chillies, chopped
250 ml cream
2 kg mussels
2 tsp dill, chopped
2 tsp parsley, snipped
50 g seaweed
lemon

Melt the butter in a large pot, add bacon and let it crisp. When the bacon is crisp add the onions and lightly caramelise with the bacon.

Add the garlic and beer and reduce by half, then add the chillies and cream.

When the cream comes to a boil, add the mussels, cover the pot and steam for 5 minutes (until all the mussels are opened).

When opened add the dill and parsley with the seaweed.

Finish with a squeeze of fresh lemon.

This recipe contains no salt because of the bacon and seaweed.

Serves 4

CALAMARI WITH TARTAR SAUCE

When I was a kid I thought calamari rings were the suckers of the octopus. Needless to say, I never ate it, even when it was on the kiddie menu at the local steakhouse in Nelspruit. My folks would order deep-fried calamari with tartar sauce but I would turn my nose up.

It was only when I started working with good, fresh seafood as a chef that I understood how good deep-fried, crumbed calamari with a thick, homemade tartar sauce could be. Fresh chokka, (calamari) from St Francis Bay is my ultimate treat. I could eat it by the bucket-load.

HOMEMADE TARTAR SAUCE
100 g gherkins, finely chopped
3 tbsp capers, finely chopped
1 medium red onion,
    finely chopped
1 clove garlic, finely chopped
2 tbsp parsley, finely chopped
100 ml fresh mayonnaise
    (page 102)
salt
pepper
1 lemon, juiced

CALAMARI
400 g calamari tubes, cleaned
salt
paprika
cayenne pepper
grated lemon zest
250 ml flour
2 eggs, lightly beaten
100 ml buttermilk
200 g panko crumbs
lemon, wedges

Place chopped gherkins and capers in a cloth and squeeze out any extra brine. Stir them with the onion, garlic and parsley into the mayonnaise. Season with salt, pepper and a squeeze of fresh lemon.

Cut the calamari into bite-size pieces. Mix a pinch each of salt, paprika and cayenne pepper into the flour and stir in the lemon zest. Pat the calamari dry and toss through the flour mixture. Use a sieve to shake off any excess flour.

Whisk the eggs and buttermilk together. Place the floured calamari into the egg and buttermilk mixture. Lift out one piece at a time, shaking off any excess mixture. Toss through the panko crumbs, making sure it is coated everywhere. Refrigerate until ready to serve.

Deep fry at 180°C until golden brown and crispy. Drain off excess oil on a paper towel.

Serve with tartar sauce and a wedge of lemon.

Serves 4

LINE FISH WITH SAUCE VIERGE

Working at Chez Bruce in London opened my eyes to so much about cooking and food. A signature Chez Bruce dish that I cooked over and over was his roast cod. It was a deceptively simple dish, and is still my favourite way to serve a line fish with firm white flesh. My version of this classic has been a feature of my cooking since those days in London.

MASH
5 large potatoes, peeled
200 ml milk
200 ml cream
200 ml olive oil
1 sprig thyme
1 sprig rosemary
2 cloves garlic
salt

FISH
4 portions hake fillet
    (about 150 g each)
coarse sea salt
vegetable oil

SAUCE VIERGE
200 g baby tomatoes, sliced
1 small red onion,
    finely chopped
1 clove garlic, crushed
1 lemon, zested and juiced
1 bunch parsley, snipped
1 handful basil, chiffonade
olive oil
salt

To make the mash, bring the potatoes to the boil from cold in a pot of salted water. Simmer uncovered until they are soft. When they are soft, strain off all the water in a colander and return the potatoes to the pot. Place the pot on the stove and shake over the heat for a few minutes so any excess moisture evaporates.

While the potatoes cook, bring the milk, cream, olive oil, thyme, rosemary and garlic to the boil in a medium saucepan. Reduce the heat and simmer for 5 minutes. Set aside so the flavours infuse.

When the potatoes are dry, work them through a food mill or rub them through a sieve with a plastic scraper. Work quickly while they are still hot. Strain the infused milk into the potatoes and whisk vigorously to incorporate. Correct the seasoning.

Incorporate more olive oil if you want the olive oil taste more pronounced. It also makes the mash firmer and shinier.

For the sauce, mix all the ingredients together. Taste to make sure the sweetness of the tomato, the acidity of the lemon juice, the herbs and seasoning all work in harmony. Set aside to infuse for up to 30 minutes while the fish is curing in the fridge.

Thicker sections of hake fillet work best for this recipe. Remove the skin, lightly sprinkle both sides of each portion with salt and place the fish on a tray in the fridge for 45 minutes. This light curing process will firm up the fish and make it easier to cook.

Remove from the fridge, wipe off any excess salt and pat dry. Heat a large non-stick pan with a generous lashing of vegetable oil, cook the hake skin-side down over moderate heat for approximately 4 minutes. When it is turned, it should have a firm golden crust. Cook for 3 minutes on the other side. (Make sure to turn the fish only once in the pan.)

Remove the pan from the heat and let the fish rest in the warm pan for a minute and a half. Serve immediately with a generous spoon of mashed potato and dress with the sauce vierge.

Serves 4

CHARRED OCTOPUS WITH GNOCCHI & NASTURTIUM PASTE

When I was first working as a chef, one of my first introductions to using 'other' ingredients in food was plating dishes with edible flowers. Nasturtiums were in the garden when I was growing up, but I never thought of them as food. Using the flowers seemed a bit ridiculous to me, but one of my team made me a salad with the leaves one day and it was delicious.

Now I use the leaves in soups and pestos and anything I can think of. Like mussels, it's an amazing food that you can find for free in your environment.

CHARRED OCTOPUS
1 small octopus, 1 – 1,2kg
1 whole chilli
2 tsp fresh ginger, whole
3 garlic cloves
6 Szechwan peppercorns
3 whole star anise
300 ml soy sauce

oil for caramelising
salt
butter for sautéing
1 lemon, zested and juiced
capers

GNOCCHI
600 g potatoes, peeled
1 egg
3 tbsp Parmesan, grated
pinch of salt
a scraping of nutmeg
150 g cake flour

Get your fishmonger to clean the octopus.

Put it in a big pot and cover with water. Add the aromatics, spices and soy sauce. Use a plate to ensure the octopus remains covered for the entire cooking process. Bring to a slow simmer and keep topping up the water as it simmers slowly for 8 hours.

When the octopus is tender, cool it in the liquid – overnight if possible.

Drain the octopus and cut into thumb-sized chunks, keeping the skin and suckers on.

For the gnocchi, peel and quarter the potatoes and place them in a pot of boiling water with a pinch of salt. When they are soft, drain, return to the pot and place back on medium heat to dry up any excess moisture.

Push the potatoes through a tammy sieve, it should yield 500 g of mashed potatoes. Mix the mash in a bowl with the egg, cheese, salt, nutmeg and flour. Ensure you mix everything through gently, to form a light dough.
Don't overwork the flour and end up with sticky gnocchi.

Bring a deep pot of salted water to a rolling boil.

On a floured surface roll the gnocchi into sausage-like cylinders about the thickness of your forefinger. Cut 2 cm lengths and gently put them into the boiling water.

When they start to float, they are ready. Remove with a slotted spoon and refresh in an ice bath.

Store on an oiled tray in the fridge until you need them.

NASTURTIUM PASTE

250 g nasturtium leaves
1 garlic clove
10 g wholegrain mustard
2 tbsp Parmesan, grated
30 g almonds, toasted
  and crushed
olive oil
salt

Make the nasturtium paste by placing the leaves in a food processor with the mustard and garlic. Pulse it to a rough textured paste, then slowly add the oil until it resembles a pesto.

Remove from the food processor and stir in the Parmesan and nuts. Add salt to taste for seasoning.

To serve, heat a generous blob of butter in a sauté pan. As soon as the butter starts foaming add 6 to 8 dumplings, and sauté until golden brown.

Season 6 octopus chunks with salt and caramelise on both sides in a hot non-stick pan with a splash of vegetable oil. Refresh with a squeeze of lemon juice. The skin should be crisp and the flesh like marrow.

Plate with dollops of nasturtium paste, fresh nasturtium leaves, lemon zest and a few fried capers for a little salty crunch.

HOME
(by die huis)

HOTEL SCRAMBLE

My dad worked in a bank. In the early days of his career, we moved a lot. We went from Cape Town to Pietersburg. Then we moved to Witbank before settling down in Nelspruit. Whenever one of these moves happened we'd stay in a local hotel while my folks found a house and schools and so on.

These weren't big, fancy city franchise hotels. They were small country places, often family-run, where the waiters wore undercoats and bowties. Melba toast was served with butter balls, and breakfast had a special flavour. It was so good.

It took me years to figure out why hotel scramble tasted different to my Ma's. I only figured it out recently: Bacon.

They cooked the scramble on flat-top grills after they did the bacon. So the bacon fat would be there for the eggs to cook in. I suppose they thought they were saving on cooking oil, not realising that a whole new dimension of flavour was being cooked into their scrambled eggs.

At home, Mareli and I have chickens. There's nothing like going out in the morning and collecting your own eggs for breakfast. It's one of those moments when you can pause and take a deep contented breath. We have a little routine. Always the same non-stick pan. Cook the bacon first, then do a slow, soft scramble in the same pan. Cooking times and tastes vary for scrambled eggs, but here's a loose recipe for my Hotel Scramble.

There's no cream, butter, créme fraiche, milk or other bullshit. It's about bacon and eggs.

6 eggs
6 rashers streaky bacon
5 ml vegetable oil
salt

Beat the eggs well with a whisk and set aside.

Buy the best bacon you can find. It really makes a difference. Heat the oil and fry the bacon in a hot pan until crisp.

Pour off the extra fat (you can use that later for cooking other things like sautéed potatoes). The pan should be coated in bacon fat. Reduce the heat to moderate and add the eggs. Fold the eggs over with a spatula, not over cooking them and keeping them moist and creamy. Quickly pour them onto your plate to avoid over cooking.

Season and serve with bacon.

It will take some practice to get them just right. But go for it, it's worth the practice.

Serves 2

GARDEN LEAF SALAD

This is one of the simplest salads to make. We are lucky enough to have a small patch of greens at our home in Stellenbosch. There is something special about picking fresh leaves for salad every night. Also, eating leaves that are traditionally not seen as salad leaves, we like things like beetroot, kale, carrot tops, nasturtium and mezuna. All different flavours and textures. We make a large batch of the dressing and keep it in a jar in the fridge to use regularly.

Garden leaves

2 tbsp wholegrain mustard
1 tbsp Dijon mustard
1 tbsp sugar
5 ml salt
1 lemon, zested and juiced
45 ml white wine vinegar
200 ml olive oil

Add all the dressing ingredients to a jar and shake vigorously to emulsify.

Toss the leaves with dressing just before serving.

Makes 250 ml dressing

VETKOEK

Vetkoek is known by different names depending on where you live. Vetkoek, fried bread or amagwenya seems to transcend cultures, and everyone knows it in one form or another.

Vetkoek filled with mince or apricot jam were a staple at church bazaars in Nelspruit. There's an auntie selling amagwenya on every station platform in the Western Cape. They are everywhere.

While I filmed Braaimaster in Lesotho, we were in this really remote place in the middle of nowhere. It was one of those times when Mareli could take some time off work and we were standing there in an icy wind, miserable and freezing our butts off. An old lady from the local village arrived with vetkoek. She had made them at home, filled them with marogo (wild spinach) and chakalaka and brought them down to offer us something warm to eat. Incredible.

That simple act of kindness, of uBuntu, lifted the mood and got the shoot rolling again. Those vetkoek tasted incredible too. It's one of my fondest memories from all the seasons of Braaimaster.

1 recipe ciabatta dough (page 82)
oil for frying

250 g salted butter
100 g apricot jam
salt
roasted almonds, crushed

Make the ciabatta dough as per the bread recipe on page 82. Leave out the coriander seeds though. You can make a couple of loaves of ciabatta and then use 2 loaves-worth of dough for making vetkoek.

Heat the oil in your deep fryer to 165°C.

After proving, turn the dough out onto a lightly floured surface. Cut into small rolls. I usually use a cookie cutter, which results in rugby-ball shaped vetkoek. As you cut, pick up the dough gently, trying not to knock out any air. This recipe yields super-light vetkoek.

Fry until golden brown then drain and cool on a wire rack.

Cream the butter with the apricot jam and salt until smooth.

Sprinkle some roasted, crushed almonds on the butter and serve with your vetkoek. This is just one option though.
You can serve these vetkoek with anything – cheese, soup, savoury mince or curry.

Serves 8 to 12

CHIP 'N DIP

There's this thing all my friends and family used to do at gatherings when I was growing up. It's a tradition that's alive and well in certain middle-class boere families today too. Whenever you go to a braai, or a get-together where they said bring-your-own, someone in the crowd would stop at the local café for chip 'n dip.

It would usually be a packet of Simba Chipniks and a tub of smooth cottage cheese with chives. Some enterprising individual might also get a packet of dried Royco French Onion soup to stir into the cottage cheese for a 'fancy' dip. Those were the days.

Back when it was 'the done thing', it seemed pretty reasonable to me. But looking back, it was quite a careless response either to the welcome of your host or the hosting of your guest. A bag of chips and a punnet of smooth cottage cheese is hardly a blip on the radar of making an effort to enjoy good company. It's kind of funny to me, and probably the reason my version of chip 'n dip takes so much time and effort. I love doing stuff like this smoked aubergine dip to share with friends or family in the course of a lekker kuier or visit.

**2–3 medium aubergines,
   sliced in half**
200 g fromage blanc
2 lemons, zested and juiced
3 cloves of garlic, sliced
150 ml olive oil
salt

Halve the aubergines and cut a grid pattern into the flesh, being careful not to pierce the skin if possible. Place them in a fireproof dish, press slivers of garlic into the cuts, then drizzle with the olive oil and salt.

Get your smoker ready and smoke the aubergine at 130°C for an hour or until the aubergines are cooked through and tender. Reserve the pan juices, and scoop the aubergine flesh out into a food processor bowl. Add the fromage blanc, lemon zest and juice and pan juices and whiz to form a nice coarse dip. Correct the seasoning and serve with your favourite vegetable chips.

Serves 6 to 8

SOUTRIBBETJIE

I never really thought much about soutribbetjie. It's a very traditional dish for sheep farming communities of the Karoo. However, for a family that got its lamb and most other meat from the supermarket, lamb ribs weren't a thing.

Like a lot of the things I now enjoy, I was introduced to the glory of soutribbetjie from a completely unexpected source. On Ultimate Braaimaster, one of the teams cooked a soutribbetjie for us to judge. It didn't look like much, but it blew my socks off. It was a recipe that gives glory to the ingredient. All you need is a rack of real Karoo lamb ribs and some salt. The awesome flavour of that lamb just shines through and leaves you sucking your fingers looking for more. The perfect soutribbetjie is a combination of herbacius Karoo lamb, moist flesh and crisp skin, with just the right amount of fat to trickle down your chin.

We cook this on the braai at home as often as we can get our hands on good quality lamb rib. Soutribbetjie needs four simple ingredients to make it great. Salt, whole lamb rib, slow coals and time. Ask your butcher to cut a whole lamb rib, including the belly and the 'lies'.

1 rack lamb ribs
⅓ cup coarse salt

Place the rib on a board and crack down the middle with a cleaver to flatten it. I'm sure your butcher will oblige. With a sharp little knife, score the fat as much as possible all over. This will help with salting and rendering the fat. Rub all over with the salt, getting it into every nook and cranny.

Secure the rib in a folding grid and hang it in a cool, dry place for at least 2 hours before cooking. The longer the better.

Make a hardwood fire with a lot of coals for long, slow cooking. This is a slow cook, and you need to turn the rib often to render out the fat. It's quite a skill, because you need to retain an even heat in the coals for an hour. You can't cook the rib too close to the coals either, as any rendered fat will flare into flames and burn your rib before it is cooked. I keep a separate fire going and top up as we go. This is a good braai dish for a long, lazy afternoon.

Serves 4

SUNDAY LUNCH

There used to be a joke about the Afrikaans kids at the English-medium school in Nelspruit. 'Why don't you phone an Afrikaner on a Sunday afternoon?'

'Because they're having Sunday lunch or sleeping it off.'

It wasn't far from the truth. It is such a tradition in middle-class South African homes to have a big roast on a Sunday and get the family around to eat it. I don't know why the English kids made the joke though, because all of them were tied up on Sundays with a huge family lunch too.

It's a wonderful tradition that I think binds families and gives them a sense of comfort and togetherness. Everyone gets to sit around eating and talking about what happened that week at school, work or in the news. There's a huge roasted joint of meat, like leg of lamb or beef topside. It makes plenty of leftovers for school lunches in the coming week.

Then there's my favourite – roast potatoes and gravy. The vegetables I used to shun, but these days they are often my favourite part. All those flavours in all those dishes made so many wonderful memories that I cherish today. It is these that sometimes guide my palate toward nostalgic flavours and combinations in the kitchen today.

Both Mareli and I have grown up with the tradition of Sunday lunch in our family and we love it. We have done our best to keep it up with friends, but with restaurant commitments it's hard. Whenever we get a chance, though, a free Sunday and a couple of mates in town with time on their hands, we slam that leg of lamb in the oven and chill the wine.

Our Sunday lunches are definitely more boozy and cheffy than the ones from our childhoods. The faces have changed and the conversation is sometimes a bit more serious, but we love them all the same.

LEG OF LAMB

1 Karoo lamb leg (2.5 kg)
3 carrots, roughly chopped
2 onions, roughly diced
handful fresh rosemary
handful fresh thyme

SALT RUB
3 tbsp course salt
2 tsp coriander seed
1 tsp black pepper, crushed
2 sprigs of rosemary, leaves
   stripped off the stalk
1 clove garlic

When you talk to your butcher about your leg of lamb, ask for it with the bone in. Ask him to remove the gland – he'll know what you are talking about. There's a little gland in the leg that makes the meat taste odd if it isn't removed before cooking.

Preheat your oven to 200°C and lay the vegetables and herbs in a roasting dish to form a sort of trivet for the lamb.

Blitz all the rub ingredients in a spice grinder or mortar and pestle to form a fine seasoning powder. Rub this generously all over the lamb and place the leg on its trivet in the roasting pan.

Place the lamb in the oven and turn it down to 175°C to roast for approximately 20 minutes per 500 g of meat – about an hour and 40 minutes. Take the leg of lamb out to rest for at least 25 minutes before carving.

Deglaze the vegetables at the bottom of the tray to make a delicious gravy.

Serves 8

OVERTURE FONDANT POTATOES

When I opened up Overture I didn't have the time, staff or space to cook potatoes for traditional fondants. We had to devise another way of making it happen, and this was the result.

1 kg baby potatoes,
    washed and halved
200 g butter
2 sprigs thyme
2 garlic cloves
salt

Melt the butter in a large skillet, and place the potatoes cut-side down in it. Season with a generous pinch of salt and slowly cook over a moderate heat. It is important to cook the potatoes slowly, for an hour, as the butter will gradually turn into beurre noisette which will lend a distinct flavour to the potatoes.

I add the thyme and garlic to the pan about halfway through the cooking process, to ensure they don't burn.

Serves 8

FORGOTTEN CARROTS

16 crisp carrots
salt and pepper
knob of butter
2 sprigs thyme
½ tsp caraway seeds

Scrub the carrots and pop them in a roasting tray. Season well with salt and pepper and dot with butter. Sprinkle with picked thyme leaves and caraway seeds, then slowly roast at 140°C. Toss and turn occasionally to glaze.

Roast for approximately an hour and a half, depending on the size of the carrots.

The forgotten bit comes from forgetting them in the oven; we roast it slowly so that the carrots candy in their own skin.

Serves 8

MARELI BAKE

I think that in all the craziness that goes on with the restaurants and the various catering and guest appearances, the conversation always seems to be about my cooking. Mareli hides her own talent in the kitchen, letting me get on with it. I think people just expect that I'm the cook in the family. Mareli can cook though, and she bakes like a dream.

In our house, baking and desserts are her thing and it's fitting that the last recipe in our first book is her recipe for my favourite cake. It also means that my wife – my strength, my companion, my partner and my love – gets the last word.

CAKE
4 egg whites
½ tsp baking powder
250 g sugar
½ tsp vanilla essence
100 g boudoir biscuits, crushed
50 g dates, chopped
100 g preserved figs, chopped
100 g pecan nuts, chopped

DECORATION
250 ml cream
2 tbsp chopped preserved figs
2 tbsp chopped pecan nuts

Beat the egg whites and baking powder in a mixer (we like Kitchen Aid) until stiff peaks form.

Add the sugar a little at a time while the beater is running, beating until glossy. Now add the vanilla and beat until incorporated. Fold the biscuits, dates, figs and pecan nuts into the egg mixture.

Preheat your oven to 160°C.

Line a standard (23 x 33 cm) Swiss roll pan with baking paper, spread the mixture onto the pan and bake for 30 minutes. Take the cake out of the oven and rest for 5 minutes before cutting it in half, paper and all, and transferring it to a wire rack to cool. Remove the paper when it is cold.

Beat the cream until stiff and spread about a third of it on the piece of the cake you choose for the base. Place the second piece of cake on top and then add the rest of the cream.

Decorate with figs and pecan nuts.

Serves 8

INDEX

GLOSSARY

Amasi A very nourishing fermented mild drink that is very popular in South Africa, served with maize porridge or as a beverage.

Biltong Leaner cuts of beef or venison, which are preserved with salt, vinegar and a combination of spices dominated by coriander. Developed to preserve hunted game meat for long treks or future use.

Boere Literally, farmers, but young Afrikaners refer to themselves as boere in a sort of self-deprecating ironic fashion.

Boerejongens Literally, farmers' children, but refers to hanepoot grapes preserved in brandy. There's a cheat version made by plumping up sultanas in brandy, but it's not the same.

Boerevrou Literally, farmer's wife, but it's a sort of back-handed compliment referring to a stern and capable Afrikaans tannie.

Boerie roll This is the South African version of the hot dog. Nice, thick, juicy piece of boerewors in a soft, white roll with fried onions. Tomato sauce and mustard are applied, but I prefer chutney.

Boerewors A traditional South African sausage that is present at every braai and almost every social gathering. It is made with beef, but often contains pork or lamb for both fat and flavour.

Bok A buck, usually springbok or impala, but a catch-all phrase for venison.

Braai The Afrikaans version of a Shisanyama where men stand around cooking meat and sausages on live coals.

Bunny chow A fantastic fast food indigenous to Durban on the country's east coast which consists of curry (the hotter the better) served in a scooped out half loaf of bread.

Chakalaka A spicy vegetable relish cooked on the stove-top or fire that is used to bring flavour to bland staples like pap or samp in especially poorer households where there isn't always meat.

Droëwors A dried version of boerewors, which tends to be made with a more intensely flavoured wors. Eaten at gatherings to watch sport, especially rugby, and prized as padkos for road-trips.

Dronkgatte Literally, drunk-arses, but usually said in jest of one's friends because, of course, Afrikaans people don't take strong drink.

Galjoen The national fish of South Africa, also known as black bream, is endemic to our coastal water and is now endangered and appears on the red list of SASSI sustainable seafood.

Kak Literally, shit, but a hold-all term for anything poor, bad, unpleasant, troublesome.

Kerk bazaar Community fund-raising events centred around the church (or kerk) which play a vital part in cementing cohesion in the Afrikaans community.

Kerrie Literally, curry, but refers specifically to curry with a specific shade of electric yellow.

Koek en tee Cake and tea gatherings where all the gossip is shared by the church tannies. The cake is always excellent. The tannies go all-out lest they be shunned.

Kos Literally food, but can also refer to comfort food, and traditional Afrikaans dishes like frikkadels and krummel pap with tamatie.

Krummel pap This is a dry, crumbly version of the staple maize porridge that is enjoyed right across the social and cultural spectrum either with gravy, tamatie sous or chakalaka.

Kuier Literally, to visit, but like so many Afrikaans words, it has a deeper meaning. To kuier properly is to sit down and really connect with someone over coffee, a meal, a wyntjie.

Kuite This is the Afrikaans word for the calf muscles on your legs, but doubles as the word for snoek roe. It's the bit fishermen take home for supper on a tough day, but can be made into a delicious treat.

Lekker Lekker means … lekker. It's a ubiquitous South African word that means 'nice', but is applied to everything by all social and cultural groups. Have a lekker day!

Melk tert Literally, milk tart, it is effectively a custard tart flavoured with cinnamon and naartjie peel.

Naartjies The loose-skinned, easy-to-peel citrus known also as a satsuma or mandarin, they are ubiquitous at rugby matches.

Oom, ouma and oupa Literally, uncle, grandmother and grandfather, but used with deference as a polite, respectful term of address for your elders and betters even if you aren't actually related.

Samp Samp is a traditional South Africa food made with corn kernels to accompany a sauce and meat.

Slap chips Literally, limp chips. Chips are cooked quickly in oil so they are limp and pale, rather than crisp and golden.

Snoek A species of snake mackerel common in South African marine fishing grounds. It is very meaty and extremely popular in poorer communities.

Soet wortels Sweet carrots are the product of the Afrikaans tradition of making vegetables palateable by adding sugar or syrup.

Soetkoekies A collective name for the little, buttery, sweet cookies that are always found in jars at ouma's house.

Spek Bacon

Tamatie sous This is a tomato sauce, the Afrikaans equivalent of chakalaka, which also has onion in it and is used for all sort of things, from frikkadel to flavouring krummel pap.

Tannie Literally, aunty, but used with deference as a polite, respectful term of address for a woman a decade or more older than you, even if you aren't actually related.

Trek Trek is a word that found its way from Afrikaans into English through the historical event known as the Great Trek. It means to move or to journey.

Tuisnywerheid Home industry. The tradition of a bunch of tannies getting together to open a shop selling their home-baked wares.

uBuntu A really South African word that means kindness, displaying humanity, compassion, welcome and warmth towards all people.

Vark Literally, pig. With the same connotation colloquially as calling someone a 'greedy pig'.

Vlek To fillet and flatten out a snoek which actually separates into 4 distinct fillets. It really is quite a skill and wonderful to watch done well.

Wyntjie Literally a 'little wine'. If you are invited for a wyntjie, it means stay for a drink.

Russel Wasserfall is a highly regarded food writer and photographer who has worked on or produced over 20 food books. His career to date includes a decade in advertising and more than a decade as an editorial and commercial food photographer.

Russel inevitably made the leap into publishing with Russel Wasserfall Food. He lives with his family in Prince Albert in the Great Karoo, where he runs an eatery with his wife, and makes bespoke cookbooks. **www.rwasserfall.co.za**

Roxy Spears lives and breathes design, and her mission is to create beautiful work and to fill the world with visual loveliness – with 25 years experience as a graphic designer, Roxy knows a thing or two about beautiful design.

Her busy studio, Good Design, has become Cape Town's go-to for food-related design. Good Design specialises in the crafted application of graphic design for food and restaurant branding, packaging design, recipe books and food truck design. **www.gooddesign.co.za**

Claire Gunn is a master of many trades. Self-taught photographer of six years, self-taught chef of 14 years, artist, blogger and stylist. She has photographed or contributed to six cookbooks: Her photography is regularly featured in South Africa's top food and lifestyle magazines, newspapers, blogs and the like.

Claire has skilfully merged her experience and passion, choosing to photograph food that is mindful, ethically farmed and sustainably sourced.
www.clairegunn.com

RWF

Editorial – Russel Wasserfall

Art direction, styling and design – Roxanne Spears of Good Design

Photography – Claire Gunn

Published by Russel Wasserfall Food, an imprint of Jacana Media (Pty) Ltd, in 2016

© Text: Russel Wasserfall, 2016
© Design: Roxanne Spears, 2016
© Photos: Claire Gunn, 2016

ISBN 978-1-928247-08-1

Jacana Media (Pty) Ltd
10 Orange Street, Sunnyside,
Auckland Park 2092,
South Africa
(+27 11) 628 3200

www.jacana.co.za

Job no. 002948
Printed and bound by ABC Press, Cape Town